Ready-to-Use
READING &
STUDY SKILLS
MASTERY
ACTIVITIES

Secondary Level

HENRIETTE L. ALLEN, Ph. D.
WALTER B. BARBE, Ph. D.
M. THERESE A. LEVESQUE, Ph. D.

**THE CENTER FOR APPLIED
RESEARCH IN EDUCATION**
West Nyack, New York 10994

Library of Congress Cataloging-in-Publication Data

Allen, Henriette L.
   Ready-to-use reading & study skills mastery activities : secondary
level / Henriette L. Allen, Walter B. Barbe, M. Therese A. Levesque.
      p.   cm.
   ISBN 0-87628-593-0
   1. Reading (Secondary)   2. Study skills.   3. Education, Secondary–
–Activity programs.   I. Barbe, Walter Burke, 1926–
II. Levesque, M. Therese A.   III. Center for Applied Research in
Education.   IV. Title.
LB1632.A54   1996   96-26401
428.4′4071′2—dc20   CIP

Printed in the United States of America

10   9   8   7   6   5   4   3   2

ISBN 0-87628-593-0

ATTENTION: CORPORATIONS AND SCHOOLS

The Center for Applied Research in Education books are available at quantity discounts with bulk purchase for educational, business, or sales promotional use. For information, please write to: Prentice Hall Special Sales, 240 Frisch Court, Paramus, New Jersey 07652. Please supply: title of book, ISBN number, quantity, how the book will be used, date needed.

THE CENTER FOR APPLIED RESEARCH IN EDUCATION
West Nyack, NY 10994
A Simon & Schuster Company

On the World Wide Web at http://www.phdirect.com

Prentice Hall International (UK) Limited, *London*
Prentice Hall of Australia Pty. Limited, *Sydney*
Prentice Hall Canada Inc., *Toronto*
Prentice Hall Hispanoamericana, S.A., *Mexico*
Prentice Hall of India Private Limited, *New Delhi*
Prentice Hall of Japan, Inc., *Tokyo*
Simon & Schuster Asia Pte. Ltd., *Singapore*
Editora Prentice Hall do Brasil, Ltda., *Rio de Janeiro*

About This Resource

Reading & Study Skills Mastery Activities: SECONDARY LEVEL is designed to give classroom teachers, reading specialists, and others who teach reading in grades 7 through 12 multiple learning activities to build specific reading skills. It includes over 200 reproducible reading and writing activities to help students master reading skills and can be used with *any* reading improvement program. The skill activities follow the sequence in the Reading Skills Check Lists developed by nationally known educator Walter B. Barbe, Ph.D. They can be assigned to individuals or groups and supervised by the teacher, a paraprofessional, parent, volunteer, or peer.

This resource offers a complete, ready-to-use teaching and management tool for building specific reading and study skills in secondary students of all ability levels, including:

1. Directions for using the reading and study skills activities to support direct instruction
2. 218 reproducible activities for quick, reliable practice or enrichment of each reading skill, with answer keys at the end
3. A reproducible Reading Skills Check List for all the major reading skill areas covered for easy individual or group recordkeeping

You will find these reading and study skills improvement activities provide:

- quick, accurate prescriptive help to meet specific reading needs
- a minimum of four ready-to-use skills exercises to reinforce and enrich instruction in each skill
- flexibility in planning individual and group activities, homework assignments, and peer- or aide-assisted instruction

The activities can be used by the teacher, parent, or reading specialist in any learning setting and in any manner the teacher deems most appropriate. They are meant to provide handy, efficient, systematic help in developing reading skills that students need to become proficient readers.

Henriette L. Allen
Walter B. Barbe
M. Therese A. Levesque

About the Authors

Henriette L. Allen, Ph.D., is a former classroom teacher in the schools of Coventry, Rhode Island, the Aramco Schools of Dhahran, Saudi Arabia, The American Community School of Benghazi, Libya, and Jackson, Mississippi. Dr. Allen served in several administrative roles, including assistant superintendent of the Jackson Public Schools. She is presently an education consultant recognized nationally.

Dr. Allen is the senior author of the series *Competency Tests for Basic Reading Skills* (West Nyack, NY: The Center for Applied Research in Education). She has taught reading skills at both elementary and secondary levels, has supervised the development of a Continuous Progress Reading Program for the Jackson Public Schools, and has lectured widely in the fields of reading, classroom management, technology in the classroom, and leadership in educational administration. Dr. Allen is listed in the *World Who's Who of Women* and *Who's Who—School District Officials*. She was the 1996 recipient of the Distinguished Service Award given by the American Association of School Administrators.

A nationally known authority in the fields of reading and learning disabilities, **Walter B. Barbe, Ph.D.,** was for twenty-five years editor-in-chief of the widely acclaimed magazine *Highlights for Children* and adjunct professor at The Ohio State University. Dr. Barbe is the author of over 150 professional articles and a number of books, including *Personalized Reading Instruction* (West Nyack, NY: Parker Publishing Co.), coauthored with Jerry L. Abbott. He is also the senior author and editor of two series—*Creative Growth with Handwriting* (Columbus, OH: Zaner-Bloser, Inc.) and *Barbe Reading Skills Check Lists and Activities* (West Nyack, NY: The Center for Applied Research in Education)—and the senior editor of *Competency Tests for Basic Reading Skills*. Dr. Barbe is a fellow of the American Psychological Association and is listed in *Who's Who in America* and *American Men of Science*.

M. Therese A. Levesque, Ph.D., has had 25 years of experience as a language teacher and administrator in the schools of Coventry, Rhode Island, and the schools of Chenango Forks and South Orangetown, New York. She has successively held positions as Language Department Chairperson, Assistant Principal, Middle School Principal, Title III Director, and Assistant Superintendent. Her activities include preparation of New York State Regents Examinations, curriculum development, and directing programs focused on reading. Dr. Levesque is presently a curriculum consultant and arbitrator for the Labor Panel of the American Arbitration Association. She is listed in *Who's Who of American Women*.

Contents

• COMPREHENSION

PART TWO

• COMPREHENSION

How to Use These Reading Skills Activities Most Effectively

The reading and study skills activities in this unit can help you make optimal use of time in helping each of your students learn to read more effectively. The first requirement for a positive learning situation is, of course, your own enthusiastic teaching. Nothing replaces that. However, the student must apply what has been taught. Instruction must be followed through. For some students, considerable practice is needed in order to be sure that the skill has not only been learned but mastered.

In order for skills to develop sequentially, it is vital that you know where a student is within the sequence of reading skills. The Reading Skills Check List and practice activities in this unit provide a practical and systematic means to meet the specific reading skill needs of each of your students on a continuing, day-to-day basis.

The reinforcement exercises offer ready-to-use opportunities to learn, practice, and master the vocabulary, word attack, comprehension, and study skills on the check list at the seventh grade level and above, including at least four pages of practice work directed to each skill. Each activity is tailored to meet the learning needs of students at the secondary level. It provides complete, easy-to-follow student directions and may be duplicated as many times as needed for individual or group use. Complete answer keys are provided at the end of the unit.

The Reading Skills Check List is *not* intended as a rigid instructional program. Rather, it is meant to offer a general pattern around which a program may be built. The check list provides specific points to verify (1) where the student is in the sequence of skills, (2) when the student masters the skills, and (3) at what rate he or she is progressing.

A reproducible copy of the Reading Skills Check List: SECONDARY LEVEL is provided on pages 12 and 13. The Check List is organized into two parts. Part One presents a summary of all of the basic vocabulary, word attack, and comprehension skills needed for effective basic reading. Part Two identifies comprehension, study skills, and creative reading skills that are more advanced or have a different emphasis. Part Two presupposes mastery of those skills in Part One.

IDENTIFYING INDIVIDUAL READING NEEDS

Before planning an instructional program for any student, it is necessary to determine at what level he or she is reading. This may be accomplished through the use of an informal reading inventory. Many such informal assessment devices are provided in *Alternative Assessment Techniques for Reading & Writing* (West Nyack, NY: The Center for Applied Research in Education, 1996), by Wilma H. Miller.

Once a student's areas of difficulty are identified, instruction can then be planned, taught, and reinforced through practice. When the student has worked through a unit of instruction, a posttest to verify mastery of the skills may be given. When mastery occurs, the student progresses to another skill. When the student is unsuccessful in a specific reading skill and a reasonable amount of instruction does not result in mastery, it may be that a different instructional method or approach is needed, or a preliminary skill needs reinforcement or remediation.

TEACHING AND REINFORCING SKILLS

After a reading skill has been identified as lacking, the teaching-learning process begins. The skill may be taught using selected literature or a reading program as the basic source of information. Explaining the skill, giving the rules which apply, and illustrating by examples are frequently used techniques. The next step in the teaching-learning process is to assign an activity with which the student can try his or her wings at learning. The activity indicates if the learning has occurred or verifies that the student understands the lesson. When the student meets that particular situation in a reading selection, he or she can apply the appropriate reading skill.

At this point in the learning process, the Reading & Study Skills Activities should become a valuable teaching asset. They include several pages of practice exercises for every reading objective on the reading skills check list as well as those found in every reading program. You can select the exercises specifically designed to aid students at their particular level of reading development. After the paper-and-pencil activities are completed—during class time, as a homework assignment, as a cooperative learning activity, or as a peer instruction activity—results of the learning activity should be discussed with the student. You can then prescribe additional practice for the skill, reteach the skill, or proceed to the next activity.

RECORDKEEPING ON THE SKILLS CHECK LIST

Recordkeeping is an important part of any instructional design. Simplicity and ease are vital. One suggested method for marking the skills check list is as follows.

II. Word Attack Skills:		
A. Knows consonant sounds	M	
1. Initial single consonants of one sound	$^8/_{20}$ M	$^8/_{28}$
2. Sounds of *c* and *g*	M	
3. Blends __ digraphs __ diphthongs __		
4. Medial sounds		
5. Final sounds		
B. Hears and can make vowel sounds		
1. Long vowels __ short vowels __		
2. Can apply vowel rules		

Put an *M* in the first column if the student takes a test and demonstrates mastery of that basic reading skill. If the student has not mastered the skill, record the date. The date in the first column then indicates when instruction in the skill began. When the student is tested a second time, put an *M* in the second column if mastery is achieved and record the date of mastery in the next column. Thus, anyone looking at the check list can tell whether the student mastered the skill before instruction or after instruction began, and when the skill was actually mastered.

Reading Skills Check List
SECONDARY LEVEL

On the following pages you will find the Reading Skills Check List: SECONDARY LEVEL. A group or individual recordkeeping form, "Class Record of Reading Skills: SECONDARY LEVEL," is also provided on pages 254–256.

Together, these forms offer a practical individual and group recordkeeping system for pinpointing students' reading progress. They provide a useful guide to instruction as well as a basis for conferences with other faculty, parents, and the student about the student's reading progress.

Reading Skills Check List
SECONDARY LEVEL*

(Last Name)   (First Name)   (Name of School)

(Age)   (Grade Placement)   (Name of Teacher)

PART ONE

I. Vocabulary:
   A. Word Recognition in Content:
   English ___
   Mathematics ___
   Social Studies ___
   Science ___
   B. Identifies Compound Words
   C. Root Words
      1. Recognizes and understands concept of root words
      2. Knows meanings of common roots
   D. Prefixes
      1. Recognizes and knows concept of prefixes
      2. Knows meanings of common prefixes:

anti-	against	antibiotic
co-	together with	cooperate
de-	down, from, away	deploy
dis-	apart from, reversing	dismantle
en-	in	encourage
ex-	out of, beyond	extrovert
pre-	before	preview
pro-	for, forward	propeller
un-	not	unkind

   E. Suffixes
      1. Recognizes and knows concept of suffixes
      2. Knows meanings of common suffixes:

-ary	place where	primary
-ist	one who acts	scientist
-ive	relating to	constructive
-less	without	fearless
-ly	similar in manner	definitely
-ment	state, quality, act	contentment
-ness	state of being	happiness
-ous	abounding in	righteous
-hood	condition of	statehood

   F. Knows meanings of terms in vocabulary of language:
      1. simile ___ metaphor ___
      2. synonym ___ antonym ___ homonym ___
      3. onomatopoeia ___

II. Word Attack Skills:
   A. Knows consonant sounds
      1. Initial single consonants of one sound
      2. Sounds of *c* and *g*
      3. Blends ___ digraphs ___ diphthongs ___
      4. Medial sounds
      5. Final sounds
   B. Hears and can make vowel sounds
      1. Long vowels ___ short vowels ___
      2. Can apply vowel rules
   C. Knows elements of syllabication
      1. Knows rules
      2. Can apply rules
   D. Uses accent properly
      1. Knows and applies rules
      2. Can shift accent and change use of word

III. Comprehension:
   A. Understands structure of story or paragraph
      1. main idea
      2. topic sentence
      3. sequence of ideas
      4. subordinate ideas
   B. Can repeat general idea of material read
   C. Can remember specific important facts
   D. Can relate material read to known information or experience
   E. Can follow printed directions
   F. Can interpret hidden meaning

PART TWO

I. Vocabulary:
   A. Increases vocabulary through wide reading
   B. Organizes own word study techniques

II. Comprehension:
   A. Interpretation
      1. Sequences events from multiple sources
      2. Makes generalizations from multiple sources
      3. Identifies relationships of elements from multiple sources
      4. Identifies author's purpose

5. Develops use of parts of speech through transformation of sequences

B. Application
1. Uses multiple sources for documentation and support for opinion
2. Uses maps, graphs, charts, tables when appropriate in response to readings
3. Takes notes during debate and other presentations in order to summarize and respond to logic used
4. Uses reading for different purposes:
   a. practical information
   b. problem solving
   c. recreation

C. Analysis
1. Differentiates between types of sentences:
   a. expository
   b. narrative
   c. descriptive
   d. persuasive

D. Synthesis
1. Extends generalizations beyond sources
2. Hypothesizes
3. Suggests alternatives and options

E. Critical Evaluation
1. Develops own criteria for critical review of materials:
   a. fiction
   b. propaganda
   c. nonfiction
   d. essays
   e. journals
   f. biographies
2. Makes judgments about author's qualifications

3. Judges reasonableness between statements and conclusions

III. Study Skills:
A. Uses thesaurus, almanac, atlas, maps, and globes
B. Uses variety of media to complete assignments and purposes
C. Uses outlining and note-taking skills
D. Adjusts reading speed to material and purpose
E. Demonstrates independence in locating, selecting, and using materials to own purpose
F. Applies problem-solving approach: identifies problem, gathers information, devises possible solutions, selects option, uses option, evaluates
G. Designs, uses, and revises own study schedules
H. Locates sources within a book by using Table of Contents and Index

IV. Creative Reading:
A. Recognizes figurative language, dialect, and colloquial speech
B. Understands literary forms:
   1. folk literature: tales, songs, fables, legends, and myths
   2. short story
   3. nonfiction, including propaganda
   4. poetry, limerick, couplet, sonnet, blank verse, and internal rhyme
C. Compares value systems of characters
D. Understands settings: social, economic, and educational
E. Responds to author's background
F. Responds to author's style of mood and point of view

Reading & Study Skills Activities
SECONDARY LEVEL

The following activities will help give students practice in the specific vocabulary, word analysis, and comprehension skills at the Secondary Level. These materials provide for the following:

- Learning opportunities for specific reading skills
- Individual and group practice and/or enrichment
- Better understanding of the classwork
- Verification of skill mastery
- Corrective exercises in specific skills
- Homework activity directed to specific reading needs
- Practice for mastery
- Optimal use of teacher time

The exercises can be photocopied just as they appear for classroom use.
Complete answer keys for activities in this resource are provided on pages 234–251.

Name: _____ Date: _____

VOCABULARY   A. Word Recognition in Content

DIRECTIONS: Many words relate to more than one subject area according to the way they are used. Study the sentences below. Each has a word underlined. To the right is a list of subject areas in which the word has a special meaning. Indicate the subject content in which the word is used by placing the letter preceding it on the space provided in front of the sentence.

_____ 1. Her beauty was the <u>magnet</u> which drew and held him.

_____ 2. In industry, electro-<u>magnets</u> have made the lifting of heavy objects easy.

_____ 3. Sodium hydroxide is a <u>caustic</u> agent.

_____ 4. <u>Caustic</u> remarks, even if made in jest, can cause irreparable harm.

_____ 5. <u>Retardation</u>, the prolonging of a tone in one chord into the following chord, produces dissonance.

_____ 6. Thanks to the Special Olympics, it is now accepted that mental <u>retardation</u> need not be a handicap to physical achievement.

_____ 7. Karl Marx is recognized as the leading <u>exponent</u> of Communism.

_____ 8. If I saw X with an <u>exponent</u> of 20, I'd give up!

_____ 9. <u>Dividends</u> are highly welcomed by stockholders.

_____ 10. To students beginning to learn division, <u>dividends</u> are a puzzlement.

a. Education
b. Music
c. Social Studies
d. Science
e. Mathematics
f. English
g. Economics

VOCABULARY   A. Word Recognition in Content

DIRECTIONS: Many words relate to more than one subject area acording to the way they are used. Study the sentences below. Each has a word underlined. To the right is a list of subject areas in which the word has a special meaning. Indicate the subject content in which the word is used by placing the letter that precedes it on the space provided in front of the sentence.

_____ 1. When the children returned to school on Monday, they were amazed to find that the solution that had been left in the pan had turned into crystals over the weekend.

      a. English
      b. Science
      c. Mathematics
      d. Social Studies

_____ 2. His meaning and intentions were made crystal clear by his gestures.

_____ 3. Addition is the first process taught in arithmetic.

_____ 4. With the addition of one element to another, chemical reactions occur.

_____ 5. Bulgaria was a satellite of Russia.

_____ 6. The moon is a satellite of the earth.

_____ 7. There is much ado about whether to call a teacher's wards pupils or students.

_____ 8. The opening in the iris of the eye through which light reaches the retina is the pupil.

_____ 9. Champaign, Illinois, is so called because it is in plain land.

_____ 10. Although very plain, she had a dignity and inner beauty that were most appealing.

VOCABULARY   A. Word Recognition in Content

DIRECTIONS: Many words relate to more than one subject area according to the way they are used. Study the sentences below. Each has a word underlined. To the right is a list of subject areas in which the word has a special meaning. Indicate the subject content in which the word is used by placing the letter preceding it on the space provided in front of the sentence.

_____ 1. His preference for <u>sharp</u> cheese was catered to by his mother.

a. Music
b. English
c. Military
d. Home Arts
e. Religion
f. Fashion
g. Food

_____ 2. With the <u>sharp</u> tool, cutting the linoleum was easy.

_____ 3. Names of accident victims are often withheld pending notification of <u>kin</u>.

_____ 4. The lute with twenty-five strings, which the Chinese girl played so beautifully, is called a <u>kin</u>.

_____ 5. Too much <u>shortening</u> put into baking ingredients can cause a cook's heartbreak.

_____ 6. Changes in women's styles regularly require <u>shortening</u> or lengthening of hems.

_____ 7. A <u>detachment</u> of the National Guard was sent to the flooded area.

_____ 8. Some individuals in monastic life practice <u>detachment</u> as a way of attaining peace.

VOCABULARY   B. Identifies Compound Words

DIRECTIONS: Write the individual words that make up the following compound words.

1. driveway   _____

2. sundeck   _____

3. blueberry   _____

4. crossbow   _____

5. doorway   _____

6. lightweight   _____

7. dishwasher   _____

8. homestead   _____

9. cheesecake   _____

10. craftsman   _____

11. campsite   _____

12. leftover   _____

13. faraway   _____

14. centerpiece   _____

15. nothing   _____

VOCABULARY   **B. Identifies Compound Words**

DIRECTIONS: Combine one of the words under A with one of those under B to form a well-known compound word. Write it under C.

	A	*B*	*C*
1.	tea	room	_____
2.	ply	shore	_____
3.	heart	top	_____
4.	air	wood	_____
5.	class	land	_____
6.	sea	bus	_____
7.	ever	port	_____
8.	hide	green	_____
9.	table	away	_____
10.	mini	spoon	_____

VOCABULARY   **B. Identifies Compound Words**

DIRECTIONS: Combine one of the words under A with one of those under B to form a well-known compound word. Write it under C.

	A	*B*	*C*
1.	cut	pan	_____
2.	home	fall	_____
3.	black	where	_____
4.	sea	out	_____
5.	water	shell	_____
6.	every	smith	_____
7.	some	mint	_____
8.	camp	made	_____
9.	pepper	day	_____
10.	sauce	stool	_____

VOCABULARY   **B. Identifies Compound Words**

DIRECTIONS: Combine a word under A with one under B to form a compound word with the meaning under C. Write the compound word under D.

		A	B	C	D
1.		after	weight	left in the mouth	_____
2.		back	side	behind the house	_____
3.		corn	by	used to thicken	_____
4.		heavy	yard	a boxer	_____
5.		time	shelf	a watch or clock	_____
6.		near	starch	contrary to far	_____
7.		book	scape	to store books	_____
8.		sail	piece	wind propelled	_____
9.		bed	taste	a doctor's manner	_____
10.		land	boat	a view	_____

VOCABULARY   C. Root Words   1. *Recognizes and understands concept of root words*

DIRECTIONS: Read the following words. On the line next to each word, write its root.

1. untrue   _____

2. wrongfully   _____

3. outweigh   _____

4. uproot   _____

5. inborn   _____

6. hangover   _____

7. habitual   _____

8. handle   _____

9. player   _____

10. expectation   _____

11. hulking   _____

12. candlelight   _____

13. handbook   _____

14. kinship   _____

VOCABULARY   C. Root Words   1. *Recognizes and understands concept of root words*

DIRECTIONS: Read the following words. On the line next to each word, write its root.

1. remodel _____

2. ceaseless _____

3. harden _____

4. hairdo _____

5. hemisphere _____

6. hemline _____

7. departure _____

8. odorless _____

9. moonrise _____

10. income _____

11. lowland _____

12. latest _____

13. midwife _____

14. expressway _____

VOCABULARY   C. Root Words   1. *Recognizes and understands concept of root words*

DIRECTIONS: Read the following words. On the line next to each word, write its root.

1. insane _____

2. irreverent _____

3. breakdown _____

4. lemonade _____

5. cowardice _____

6. chargeable _____

7. hardness _____

8. handicap _____

9. mildness _____

10. mythical _____

11. encampment _____

12. hemicycle _____

13. headline _____

14. rental _____

VOCABULARY   **C. Root Words**   **1.** *Recognizes and understands concept of root words*

DIRECTIONS: Read the following words. On the line next to each word, write its root.

1. herdsman _____

2. homely _____

3. unwell _____

4. gasometer _____

5. outrun _____

6. uplift _____

7. judgeship _____

8. confirmation _____

9. cannonade _____

10. canalize _____

11. bimonthly _____

12. grandeur _____

13. inactive _____

14. handful _____

VOCABULARY   C. Root Words   2. *Knows meanings of common root words*

DIRECTIONS: The groups of words below share a common root. Look up each of these words in a dictionary to learn its meaning, especially the meaning of its root. Underline the root. Write the definition of the word.

1. a. audible   _____

    b. audiometer   _____

    c. audiologist   _____

    d. audition   _____

    e. audiogram   _____

2. a. phonetics   _____

    b. phonic   _____

    c. phonics   _____

    d. phonograph   _____

    e. phonetician   _____

3. a. polygon   _____

    b. polygamy   _____

    c. polynominal   _____

    d. polytechnic   _____

    e. polypod   _____

4. a. philosopher   _____

    b. philharmonic   _____

    c. philanthropist _____

    d. philanthropy   _____

    e. philosophy   _____

Name: _____ Date: _____

DIRECTIONS: The groups of words below share a common root. Look up each of these words in a dictionary to learn its meaning, especially the meaning of its root. Underline the root. Write the definition of the word.

1. a. ocular   _____

    b. oculist   _____

    c. binocular   _____

2. a. telegram   _____

    b. telephone   _____

    c. telescope   _____

    d. television   _____

    e. telepathy   _____

3. a. solid   _____

    b. solidarity   _____

    c. solidify   _____

    d. solidity   _____

4. a. parasol   _____

    b. solar   _____

    c. solarium   _____

    d. solstice   _____

VOCABULARY   **C. Root Words**   **2. *Knows meanings of common root words***

DIRECTIONS: The groups of words below share a common root. Look up each of these words in a dictionary to learn its meaning, especially the meaning of its root. Underline the root. Write the definition of the word.

1. a. petrol _____

    b. petrify _____

    c. petrogram _____

    d. petrous _____

    e. petroleum _____

2. a. gerontology _____

    b. gerontocracy _____

    c. geriatrics _____

    d. geriatrist _____

3. a. pedal _____

    b. pedestrian _____

    c. pedicure _____

    d. pedometer _____

    e. pedestal _____

    f. impede _____

4. a. centenary _____

    b. centennial _____

    c. centigrade _____

    d. centipede _____

    e. centimeter _____

    f. centigram _____

VOCABULARY   C. Root Words   2. *Knows meanings of common root words*

DIRECTIONS: The group of words below share a common root. Look up each of these words in a dictionary to learn its meaning, especially the meaning of its root. Underline the root. Write the definition of the word.

1. a. geocentric   _____

    b. geochemistry _____

    c. geodesy   _____

    d. geography   _____

    e. geology   _____

2. a. photography   _____

    b. photoelectric   _____

    c. photometer   _____

    d. photomicroscope _____

    e. photophone   _____

3. a. soliloquy   _____

    b. solitaire   _____

    c. solitude   _____

    d. solo   _____

    e. soloist   _____

4. a. biology   _____

    b. biography   _____

    c. biometry   _____

    d. biochemistry _____

    e. biotype   _____

VOCABULARY   D. Prefixes   1. *Recognizes and knows concept of prefixes*

DIRECTIONS: For each word below that has a prefix, write the prefix on the line next to the word. If there is no prefix, leave the line blank.

1. antidote   _____

2. precede   _____

3. derby   _____

4. coauthor   _____

5. deplane   _____

6. preen   _____

7. enfold   _____

8. antique   _____

9. projection   _____

10. exceed   _____

VOCABULARY   D. Prefixes   1. *Recognizes and knows concept of prefixes*

DIRECTIONS: For each word below that has a prefix, write the prefix on the line next to the word. If there is no prefix, leave the line blank.

1. cocoa   _____

2. prepaid   _____

3. enjoy   _____

4. disobey   _____

5. tranquil   _____

6. irrelevant   _____

7. understudy   _____

8. upright   _____

9. surmount   _____

10. surely   _____

VOCABULARY   D. Prefixes   1. *Recognizes and knows concept of prefixes*

DIRECTIONS: Circle any prefixes in the words below.

1. presentiment

2. profound

3. imminent

4. decadence

5. exceptional

6. enforce

7. exercise

8. precious

9. inane

10. coherent

VOCABULARY   D. Prefixes   1. *Recognizes and knows concept of prefixes*

DIRECTIONS: Circle any prefixes in the words below.

1. enclose

2. disciple

3. discount

4. interest

5. preclude

6. cohabit

7. example

8. discord

9. enemy

10. antipathy

VOCABULARY   D. Prefixes   2. *Knows meanings of common prefixes*

DIRECTIONS: In the space provided, write the prefix that will give the meaning indicated in the right-hand column.

1. _____ equal   equal together

2. _____ freeze   against freezing in a radiator

3. _____ ceed   go beyond

4. _____ lude   music played before

5. _____ miss   send away from

6. _____ tour   go around; go away from

7. _____ ter   go into

8. _____ pel   drive forward

9. _____ ter   keep from; turn from

10. _____ pose   put forward; suggest

11. _____ qualify   declare unfit

12. _____ fer   change over

13. _____ histamine   a drug against allergy

14. _____ snare   trap

15. _____ timely   not the right time

VOCABULARY   D. Prefixes   2. *Knows meanings of common prefixes*

DIRECTIONS: In the space provided, write the prefix that will give the meaning indicated in the right-hand column.

1. _____ just   not just

2. _____ judge (judice)   judge before; judgment made before

3. _____ Communist   against Communism

4. _____ dawn   before dawn

5. _____ vide   see ahead; forward; for the future

6. _____ necessary   not necessary

7. _____ pel   push out of

8. _____ pel   push apart; from

9. _____ worker   one who works together with

10. _____ mote   put down

11. _____ camp   break camp; depart from

12. _____ roll   put a name on a roll or register

There are several prefixes all of which mean *not*:

un- in- ir- il- im-

Put the correct prefix before each word that follows to give it a negative meaning.

a. _____ legal   e. _____ mortal   i. _____ logical

b. _____ religious f. _____ ert   j. _____ mature

c. _____ active   g. _____ regular   k. _____ pertinent

d. _____ worthy   h. _____ clean   l. _____ reversible

VOCABULARY   **D. Prefixes**   **2.** *Knows meanings of common prefixes*

DIRECTIONS: In each sentence below, fill in the blank with a word that has a prefix and has the meaning indicated by the phrase in parentheses that follows the sentence.

1. To _____ the refrigerator is a tedious job.
   (take the frost from)

2. Joining hands, the children _____ their teacher.
   (put in a circle)

3. To avoid war, we must make every effort to _____ with nations who dislike us.
   (live; exist together with)

4. Dr. George said, "Inhale. Good! Now, _____ ."
   (breathe out)

5. A sign at the pond said "_____ for Skating" because the weather had been warm.
   (not safe)

6. We will _____ with the meeting as soon as everyone is here.
   (go ahead with)

7. To predict the outcome so early in the season is somewhat _____ .
   (too early)

8. Against some poisons, milk is a good _____ .
   (against poison)

9. Their best quarterback was declared _____ to play for the rest of the season.
   (not fit)

10. The date for end-of-the-year graduation is _____ in September.
    (set in advance)

VOCABULARY   D. Prefixes   2. *Knows meanings of common prefixes*

DIRECTIONS: Give a meaning for the underlined word which will show that you know the meaning of the prefix.

1. We were compelled to <u>postpone</u> our departure by the inclement weather.

   _____

2. Never <u>underestimate</u> your own ability.

   _____

3. More and more cities are acquiring <u>subways</u> for mass transit.

   _____

4. It was her <u>misfortune</u> to be on the scene at the time of the accident.

   _____

5. The heavy rains caused the reservoir to <u>overflow</u>.

   _____

6. <u>Unemployment</u> is a cause of concern for the individuals involved and society as a whole.

   _____

7. His <u>involvement</u> in politics has been lifelong.

   _____

8. The Concorde jet has cut the time for <u>transoceanic</u> travel in half.

   _____

9. Not to be <u>outdone</u>, he tried harder and spent more.

   _____

10. There are space satellites <u>circumnavigating</u> the earth.

    _____

VOCABULARY   E. Suffixes   1. *Recognizes and knows concept of suffixes*

DIRECTIONS: Circle any suffixes in the words below.

1. suddenly

2. economize

3. depart

4. abandonment

5. edible

6. precede

7. comedian

8. sponsorship

9. overexert

10. helpless

VOCABULARY   E. Suffixes   **1. *Recognizes and knows concept of suffixes***

DIRECTIONS: Circle any suffixes in the words below.

1. predicament

2. transfer

3. responsive

4. wickedly

5. position

6. boyish

7. salable

8. provoke

9. auditory

10. refugee

VOCABULARY   E. Suffixes   1. *Recognizes and knows concept of suffixes*

DIRECTIONS: Circle any suffixes in the words below.

1. friendship

2. absent

3. violinist

4. substitute

5. responsive

6. demonstrate

7. portable

8. silken

9. proposal

10. bestiary

VOCABULARY   E. Suffixes   1. *Recognizes and knows concept of suffixes*

DIRECTIONS: Circle any suffixes in the words below.

1. worthless

2. odorous

3. aviary

4. herdsman

5. girlhood

6. outrage

7. shyness

8. singly

9. misdeed

10. foretell

VOCABULARY **E. Suffixes** **2. *Knows meanings of common suffixes***

DIRECTIONS: Add a suffix to give the meaning indicated in the right-hand column.

1. frivol _____ abounding in frivolity

2. mother _____ condition of being a mother

3. hard _____ state of being hard

4. adorn _____ act of adorning

5. man _____ like a man

6. hat _____ without a hat

7. sport _____ relating to sports

8. continu _____ without interruption

9. spite _____ full of spite

10. employ _____ object of employing

VOCABULARY   E. Suffixes   2. *Knows meanings of common suffixes*

DIRECTIONS: Select and circle the suffix that gives the meaning indicated to a root word.

1. condition of being a mother
   -hood   -able   -ee   -ish

2. abounding in danger
   -able   -ness   -ous   -less

3. place where birds or bees (for example) are kept
   -ist   -ary   -ive   -oid

4. without
   -ment   -ness   -hood   -less

5. state of being content
   -ment   -ly   -ist   -ize

6. one who practices or is concerned with a piano
   -hood   -ist   -ish   -ship

7. like or similar to a woman
   -ive   -less   -ly   -ist

8. tendency to or disposition for action
   -ive   -able   -ness   -ee

9. state of being good
   -ive   -able   -ness   -ee

10. condition, character, or office of king
    -hood   -ist   -ee   -ship

VOCABULARY   E. Suffixes   2. *Knows meanings of common suffixes*

DIRECTIONS: Write a suffix to give the meaning indicated in the right-hand column.

1. principal   _____   office of principal

2. saint   _____   condition of being a saint

3. guile   _____   without guile

4. saxophone   _____   one who plays the saxophone

5. act   _____   tendency to act

6. wet   _____   state of being wet

7. languor   _____   abounding in languor

8. discontent   _____   state of being discontent

9. kin   _____   condition of being kin

10. credi   _____   ability to be believed

VOCABULARY   **E. Suffixes**   **2.** *Knows meanings of common suffixes*

DIRECTIONS: In the sentences below, fill in each blank with a word that has a suffix and the meaning indicated at the end of the sentence.

1. The president was again the _____ of his party.
   (object of being nominated)

2. He spoke as if he were _____ .
   (without aim)

3. Youth is often more _____ than are older people.
   (tending to keep things unchanged)

4. Everyone appreciated the _____ of his speech.
   (state of being direct)

5. His illness has made him unable to seek _____ .
   (being employed)

6. Our band director is also a professional _____ .
   (person who plays the flute)

7. Bob was _____ that we be comfortable.
   (full of solicitude)

8. Some physical exercises are more _____ than helpful.
   (full of harm)

9. To _____ the crisis stage, severe steps were taken.
   (make short)

10. That question has been decided; it is no longer _____ .
    (able to be debated)

VOCABULARY   F. Knows Meanings of Terms in   1. *Simile, metaphor*
                 Vocabulary of Language

DIRECTIONS: Read the following sentences carefully. Underline the simile or metaphor. On the line provided, write *S* if the underlined phrase is a simile and *M* if it is a metaphor.

1. _____   The hair on his head was as white as wool.

2. _____   "They're growing like weeds," the mother remarked to her husband as they watched their children playing.

3. _____   Ponce de Leon has many followers seeking his elusive fountain of youth.

4. _____   Flat on his back, hidden in the tall grass, he was the sole spectator at the ballet of the clouds gracefully crossing the stage of the summer sky.

5. _____   On that snowy winter day before vacation, the noise in the cafeteria hit the ears of the adults like the din of a rock concert.

6. _____   Her sharp comment cracked and hit like a whip.

7. _____   Although he fought bravely, he lost his duel with death.

8. _____   Their smiles sang their welcome.

9. _____   With the reopening of the mines, prosperity spread over the town like a welcome dew.

10. _____   The beauty of the rose was hers.

VOCABULARY   **F. Knows Meanings of Terms in**   1. *Simile, metaphor*
              Vocabulary of Language

DIRECTIONS: Read the following sentences carefully. Underline the simile or metaphor. On the line provided, write *S* if the underlined phrase is a simile and *M* if it is a metaphor.

1. _____   With oxen strength, he lifted the fallen tree to free the victim.

2. _____   A stream of words flowed from her heart, too long dammed by the silence of solitude.

3. _____   When Mary dropped her doll, her hands remained lifted and as empty as those of a mother who has lost her beloved child.

4. _____   The joy of success is as intoxicating as wine.

5. _____   In her garden, roses awakened with every day.

6. _____   The vineyard owner gazing at his acres of fruit saw them as ruby liquid in crystal settings.

7. _____   His inheritance disappeared like snow in the desert.

8. _____   Eyes open the door of morning and close the door of night.

9. _____   They watched the slowly flowing stream caressing the shore.

10. _____   She came and went like the wind.

VOCABULARY   **F. Knows Meanings of Terms in**   **1.** *Simile, metaphor*
                   Vocabulary of Language

DIRECTIONS: Read the following sentences carefully. Underline the simile or metaphor. On the line provided, write *S* if the underlined phrase is a simile and *M* if it is a metaphor.

1. _____   Her beauty was as placid as a water lily.

2. _____   Time slips beneath our feet.

3. _____   Youth yearns to taste to the full the wine of life.

4. _____   Old age finds it wise to divorce the foolishness of youth.

5. _____   In moments of detached contemplation, life often seems like a magic shadow show.

6. _____   Her tears in the end washed away her grief.

7. _____   A reputation is often sold for a bribe.

8. _____   Our star wrestler has legs like hams.

9. _____   The rain on the metal roof sounded like a tap dance in double time.

10. _____   The street lights gleamed like dragon eyes.

VOCABULARY   **F. Knows Meanings of Terms in**   **1. *Simile, metaphor***
                               Vocabulary of Language

DIRECTIONS: Read the following sentences carefully. Underline the simile or metaphor. On the line provided, write *S* if the underlined phrase is a simile and *M* if it is a metaphor.

1. _____   After the summer drought, the thirsty earth gulped down the torrential rain.

2. _____   For the awe-struck child, the world's tallest building touched the sky.

3. _____   The sun that day set in a fiery furnace glow.

4. _____   The sky darkened and frowned and then let out a thunderous roar.

5. _____   When the sick child finally smiled, it was as if someone had turned on a light.

6. _____   Seen from the window of the twentieth floor, the city rooftops were a crazy quilt of somber colors.

7. _____   Their jiving and dancing made them look like dervishes walking on hot coals.

8. _____   For a child, time is a creeper; for a youth, it is a jogger; for an aged person, time is a sprinter.

9. _____   Furious, he pivoted on his frustration.

10. _____   The news that war had been declared was like a hook in the heart.

VOCABULARY **F. Knows Meanings of Terms in** **2.** *Synonym, antonym,*
Vocabulary of Language *homonym*

DIRECTIONS: Read the following pairs of words. On the line provided, write *S* for synonyms, *A* for antonyms, and *H* for homonyms.

1. _____ doldrums—hurricane

2. _____ respectful—insolent

3. _____ sultry—stuffy

4. _____ logical—irrational

5. _____ trouble—matter

6. _____ challenge—dare

7. _____ wait—weight

8. _____ apology—accusation

9. _____ seed—cede

10. _____ peak—peek

Name: _____ Date: _____

DIRECTIONS: Read the following pairs of words. On the line provided, write *S* for synonyms, *A* for antonyms, and *H* for homonyms.

1. _____ knot—not

2. _____ merriment—gloom

3. _____ bastion—fortress

4. _____ nominate—designate

5. _____ pedal—peddle

6. _____ bleak—cheery

7. _____ hew—hue

8. _____ enlarge—reduce

9. _____ require—need

10. _____ harbinger—herald

VOCABULARY   **F. Knows Meanings of Terms in**   **2.** *Synonym, antonym,*
                 Vocabulary of Language   *homonym*

DIRECTIONS: Read the following pairs of words. On the line provided, write *S* for synonyms, *A* for antonyms, and *H* for homonyms.

1. _____ pardon—forgive

2. _____ hoard—squander

3. _____ fact—fiction

4. _____ wood—would

5. _____ prove—demonstrate

6. _____ face—visage

7. _____ barren—fertile

8. _____ fowl—foul

9. _____ waist—waste

10. _____ revise—correct

DIRECTIONS: Read the following pairs of words. On the line provided, write *S* for synonyms, *A* for antonyms, and *H* for homonyms.

1. _____ behead—decapitate

2. _____ punish—chastise

3. _____ conceal—disclose

4. _____ meddle—medal

5. _____ defame—praise

6. _____ defend—protect

7. _____ great—grate

8. _____ here—hear

9. _____ desire—want

10. _____ prosecute—defend

VOCABULARY   **F. Knows Meanings of Terms in**   3. *Onomatopoeia*
                   Vocabulary of Language

DIRECTIONS: Underline any onomatopoetic expressions in the following sentences.

1. Silence reigned until the telephone rang.

2. Arduously, the weak and aged man slowly shuffled in his sagging house slippers.

3. He fought against the swish, swish, swish of the window wipers putting him to sleep.

4. The pneumatic drill's repeated jagged whirring crowded out every other street sound.

5. The ship's loud whistle blasted everyone out of their wits.

6. Her taffeta dress rustled to the rhythm of her dancing.

7. Now murmuring, now sighing, the pine trees responded to the wind.

8. As we approached the hives, the buzzing of the bees busy at their task gradually engulfed us.

9. A mere ripple of applause warned the comedian that his joke had fallen flat.

10. Drums, draped in black, sounded out their last farewell in a muffled, mournful beat.

VOCABULARY   **F. Knows Meanings of Terms in   3. *Onomatopoeia***
              Vocabulary of Language

DIRECTIONS: Underline any onomatopoetic expressions in the following sentences.

1. We knew by its lonely baying at the moon that the coyote was near.

2. Barking, helping, and yawping welcomed us to the dog pound.

3. A half-detached muffler jangled as it played tag with the road.

4. The bull bellowed and the cow mooed.

5. One's first experience of hearing women chanting in wailing ululation causes culture shock.

6. On the street corner, a hand organ was grinding out a merry, wheezing, tinny tune.

7. "Tanrantara, tanrantara, tanrantara," the trumpets sang.

8. In the background, the bull fiddler plucked and bowed his rhythmic bass.

9. Did you ever drive with freezing rain and sleet bruising, beating, and punishing your car?

10. They found their way to the party room by tracking down the glasses clinking and the voices rising.

VOCABULARY   **F. Knows Meanings of Terms in**   3. *Onomatopoeia*
              Vocabulary of Language

DIRECTIONS: Underline any onomatopoetic expressions in the following sentences.

1. Wailing sirens in the still night tell of disaster befalling someone.

2. The television sportscaster says "Boom!" every time someone hits a ball.

3. The "caw caw" of a lone crow was the accompaniment to which she picked blueberries.

4. The sudden, long hissing of the slithering snake startled her.

5. The tired and worn-out lawn mower just putt-putted along.

6. What warming memories are awakened by the tintinnabulation of all those sleigh bells!

7. The engine that the brother and sister were trying to get going sputtered to silent immobility.

8. Announcement of the shower's end came from the lazy drip, drip, drip of the rainwater from the eaves.

9. Jolted, he dropped the tray of ice cubes, and the ice beat out an abrupt tattoo in the sink.

10. Fear intensified the pounding of her heart, blocking out every other sound.

VOCABULARY   **F. Knows Meanings of Terms in**   **3.** *Onomatopoeia*
                         Vocabulary of Language

DIRECTIONS: Underline any onomatopoetic expressions in the following sentences.

1. Prolonged and varied meows of the cats' concert upset the stillness of the night.

2. Morning was announced by the red rooster's long and joyous cock-a-doodle-doo.

3. Crackling, crepitant, the fire glowed to warm and cheer us all.

4. The young audience giggled uncomfortably.

5. At the scratching of a fingernail on the blackboard, his back prickled.

6. Weeping willows wilted sadly in the burning heat.

7. The sleeping cat purred in its sleep.

8. I see and hear a picture every time I sing "bombs bursting in air."

9. The bat hit the ball with a resounding crack and broke.

10. A giggling gaggle of girls infected all those around them with smiles.

WORD ATTACK   A. Knows Consonant Sounds   1. *Initial single consonants of one sound*

DIRECTIONS: Read the list of words carefully. Group the words by initial single consonant.

vow	gorgeous	gate
darling	massive	jaunty
jangle	nominee	daffodil
view	mayonnaise	gorge
follicle	gadfly	headless
master	fertile	jury
fancy	noble	derelict
nightmare	holster	visage
hearing	jail	noise

WORD ATTACK   **A. Knows Consonant Sounds**   **1.** *Initial single consonants of one sound*

DIRECTIONS: Read the list of words carefully. Group the words by initial single consonant.

solar	rivulet	kettle
winner	mimic	roar
kicker	solicitude	would
modern	jack	muster
lodestone	kitten	listless
jade	sirloin	rue
rousing	modality	joke
jargon	livery	sixty
wild	winter	linchpin

_____

_____

_____

_____

_____

_____

_____

WORD ATTACK   **A. Knows Consonant Sounds**   1. *Initial single consonants of one sound*

DIRECTIONS: Read the list of words carefully. Group the words by initial single consonant.

pension	sour	nunnery
home	heredity	tenacious
salary	precious	hateful
balcony	hike	bachelor
number	tentative	pansy
balsam	nurse	sentence
puddle	bagpipe	facile
folly	salesman	teacher
tender	foreign	novel

_____

_____

_____

_____

_____

_____

_____

WORD ATTACK   A. Knows Consonant Sounds   1. *Initial single consonants of one sound*

DIRECTIONS: Read the list of words carefully. Group the words by initial single consonant.

care	falter	ginger
geography	kidney	luster
bicycle	consonant	fellow
kinsman	luncheon	kale
bottom	giant	cartoon
pillar	bothersome	pullet
tear	beep	likely
false	lithesome	giraffe
lump	pulse	bother

_____

_____

_____

_____

_____

_____

_____

_____

WORD ATTACK   **A. Knows Consonant Sounds**   **2. *Sounds of c and g***

DIRECTIONS: Write each word in the space provided, using the correct spelling.

_____ 1. gī

_____ 2. kal′ sē əm

_____ 3. giv

_____ 4. kō′ kō

_____ 5. ə gō′

_____ 6. gag

_____ 7. kaf

_____ 8. des′ ə m'l

_____ 9. kärd

_____ 10. myōō′ zik

_____ 11. dij′ it

_____ 12. fās

_____ 13. kab

_____ 14. keg

_____ 15. di sīd′

_____ 16. rē′ jən

_____ 17. jə raf′

_____ 18. bag′ ij

_____ 19. kān

_____ 20. gōl

Name: _____ Date: _____

WORD ATTACK   A. Knows Consonant Sounds   2. *Sounds of* c *and* g

DIRECTIONS: Write each word in the space provided, using the correct spelling.

_____ 1. jip	_____ 11. dēk′ ′n
_____ 2. kad	_____ 12. kə det′
_____ 3. jem	_____ 13. jē
_____ 4. dān′ jər	_____ 14. rānj
_____ 5. gāz	_____ 15. di kamp′
_____ 6. kāj	_____ 16. kāk
_____ 7. jē äm′ ə trē	_____ 17. jin′ jər
_____ 8. krit′ik	_____ 18. bag
_____ 9. di′ koi	_____ 19. ā′ jid
_____ 10. glad	_____ 20. kam′ ər a

WORD ATTACK   A. Knows Consonant Sounds   2. *Sounds of* c *and* g

DIRECTIONS: Write each word in the space provided, using the correct spelling.

_____ 1. si ment′

_____ 2. ri sīt′

_____ 3. gō

_____ 4. fakt

_____ 5. peg

_____ 6. sər′ k'l

_____ 7. ē′ gō

_____ 8. kut

_____ 9. gāj

_____ 10. sil′ ən dər

_____ 11. sī′ k'l

_____ 12. tī′ gər

_____ 13. sīt

_____ 14. eg

_____ 15. gôlf

_____ 16. en′ jən

_____ 17. gäth′ ik

_____ 18. sī′ fər

_____ 19. sāj

_____ 20. grēf

WORD ATTACK   **A. Knows Consonant Sounds**   **2. *Sounds of c and g***

DIRECTIONS: Write each word in the space provided, using the correct spelling.

_____	1. sər′ kəs	_____	11. kus
_____	2. gāt	_____	12. jē äl′ ə jē
_____	3. jərm	_____	13. get
_____	4. sel	_____	14. gōst
_____	5. jent′ ′l	_____	15. siv′ ′l
_____	6. gərl	_____	16. jər′ mən
_____	7. kōd	_____	17. gut
_____	8. āj	_____	18. si gär′
_____	9. dig′ ər	_____	19. ē käl′ ə jē
_____	10. lag	_____	20. pij′ ən

WORD ATTACK   A. Knows Consonant Sounds   3. a. *Blends*

DIRECTIONS: Many small words and syllables are made up of a vowel and a cluster of consonant letters on each side. Because these clusters of consonants are pronounced together, or blended, they seem to make one sound and are called *consonant blends*. Underline the consonant blends in the following words.

1. frog

2. retread

3. swallow

4. regret

5. sky

6. platoon

7. anklet

8. respect

9. enclosure

10. encumbrance

11. black

12. glimpse

13. triple

14. draft

15. reprieve

16. glove

17. silverplated

18. brat

19. risky

20. refresh

WORD ATTACK   A. Knows Consonant Sounds   3. a. *Blends*

DIRECTIONS: Many small words and syllables are made up of a vowel and a cluster of consonant letters on each side. Because these clusters of consonants are pronounced together, or blended, they seem to make one sound and are called *consonant blends*. Underline the consonant blends in the following words.

1. crystal

2. frisk

3. between

4. scornful

5. prattle

6. shopper

7. dribble

8. rewrite

9. acclimate

10. conglomerate

11. twirler

12. saffron

13. speculate

14. ungrateful

15. abscond

16. wrought

17. astute

18. effluvial

19. bookplate

20. swirl

WORD ATTACK   A. Knows Consonant Sounds   3. a. *Blends*

DIRECTIONS: Many small words and syllables are made up of a vowel and a cluster of consonant letters on each side. Because these clusters of consonants are pronounced together, or blended, they seem to make one sound and are called *consonant blends*. Underline the consonant blends in the following words.

1. spatter

2. sharecropper

3. ingrate

4. snag

5. anglicize

6. approval

7. drumfire

8. blooming

9. flowery

10. occlude

11. dragon

12. besmirch

13. abbreviate

14. employment

15. static

16. retreat

17. swelter

18. congregate

19. overwrought

20. freedom

Name: _____ Date: _____

DIRECTIONS: Many small words and syllables are made up of a vowel and a cluster of consonant letters on each side. Because these clusters of consonants are pronounced together, or blended, they seem to make one sound and are called *consonant blends*. Underline the consonant blends in the following words.

1. refrain

2. English

3. crustacean

4. egret

5. plotted

6. dweller

7. Africa

8. breach

9. drought

10. wrecker

11. cluster

12. trooper

13. prudent

14. smile

15. glorious

16. angler

17. despise

18. rheostat

19. swimming

20. ablution

WORD ATTACK   A. Knows Consonant Sounds   3. b. *Digraphs*
                                                    c. *Diphthongs*

DIRECTIONS: Consonant letters that combine to form a new sound are called a *digraph*. A *diphthong* is the sound made by gliding continuously between two vowels within the same syllable, like *oy* in *boy*.

Read the words below. Underline the digraphs and the diphthongs. On the blank lines, write "a" if the underlined letters form a digraph and "b" if they form a diphthong. If more than one digraph or diphthong occur in a word, write "a" or "b" in the order in which they occur in the word.

_____ 1. empathy   _____ 11. graph

_____ 2. foe   _____ 12. soybean

_____ 3. phosphorous   _____ 13. path

_____ 4. voile   _____ 14. snail

_____ 5. fish   _____ 15. poison

_____ 6. peace   _____ 16. shush

_____ 7. thrush   _____ 17. glue

_____ 8. juice   _____ 18. soil

_____ 9. chore   _____ 19. shuffle

_____ 10. wish   _____ 20. pharmacy

WORD ATTACK   **A. Knows Consonant Sounds   3.   b. *Digraphs***
                                                  c. *Diphthongs*

DIRECTIONS: Consonant letters that combine to form a new sound are called a *digraph*. A *diphthong* is the sound made by gliding continuously between two vowels within the same syllable, like *oy* in *boy*.

Read the words below. Underline the digraphs and the diphthongs. On the blank lines, write "a" if the underlined letters form a digraph and "b" if they form a diphthong. If more than one digraph or diphthong occur in a word, write "a" or "b" in the order in which they occur in the word.

_____   1. eater   _____   11. chicanery

_____   2. itch   _____   12. relieve

_____   3. royal   _____   13. coy

_____   4. phrase   _____   14. physics

_____   5. quail   _____   15. shameful

_____   6. shapely   _____   16. toil

_____   7. daub   _____   17. bonsai

_____   8. Shoshone   _____   18. whorl

_____   9. cue   _____   19. recoil

_____   10. phantom   _____   20. shore

WORD ATTACK   A. Knows Consonant Sounds   3. b. *Digraphs*
                                                c. *Diphthongs*

DIRECTIONS: Consonant letters that combine to form a new sound are called a *digraph*. A *diphthong* is the sound made by gliding continuously between two vowels within the same syllable, like *oy* in *boy*.

Read the words below. Underline the digraphs and the diphthongs. On the blank lines, write "a" if the underlined letters form a digraph and "b" if they form a diphthong. If more than one digraph or diphthong occur in a word, write "a" or "b" in the order in which they occur in the word.

_____ 1. noise

_____ 2. church

_____ 3. sea

_____ 4. photo

_____ 5. pail

_____ 6. whey

_____ 7. coat

_____ 8. shout

_____ 9. receive

_____ 10. slush

_____ 11. thistle

_____ 12. philosopher

_____ 13. lie

_____ 14. therefore

_____ 15. catch

_____ 16. daily

_____ 17. onomatopoeia

_____ 18. thresh

_____ 19. crowd

_____ 20. cause

WORD ATTACK   **A. Knows Consonant Sounds   3. b.** *Digraphs*
                                            c. *Diphthongs*

DIRECTIONS: Consonant letters that combine to form a new sound are called a *digraph*. A *diphthong* is the sound made by gliding continuously between two vowels within the same syllable, like *oy* in *boy*.

Read the words below. Underline the digraphs and the diphthongs. On the blank lines, write "a" if the underlined letters form a digraph and "b" if they form a diphthong. If more than one digraph or diphthong occur in a word, write "a" or "b" in the order in which they occur in the word.

_____	1. cease	_____	11. chicken
_____	2. bathe	_____	12. either
_____	3. pie	_____	13. load
_____	4. what	_____	14. whimper
_____	5. nail	_____	15. phonics
_____	6. rhythm	_____	16. rail
_____	7. toil	_____	17. thyroid
_____	8. faith	_____	18. haul
_____	9. deceive	_____	19. phosphorous
_____	10. poise	_____	20. porpoise

WORD ATTACK   **A. Knows Consonant Sounds**   4. *Medial sounds*

DIRECTIONS: From the following lists, find three words that have the medial consonant indicated in the left column. Write these words on the line opposite that consonant.

inherit	haying	banker	candy	baseball
footing	beefy	hollow	staging	goner
tanker	debit	halyard	rehire	infect
index	payee	maggot	pony	celery
suited	seeking	wherefore	raider	slumber
ceiling	behold	cogitate	sentence	panic

n _____

y _____

l _____

t _____

h _____

f _____

k _____

g _____

d _____

b _____

WORD ATTACK   **A. Knows Consonant Sounds**   **4. *Medial sounds***

DIRECTIONS: From the following lists, find three words that have the medial consonant indicated in the left column. Write these words on the line opposite that consonant.

carbon	logic	careful	content	tonal
ticket	sailor	afire	befit	foyer
tidy	reheat	debut	peeker	mayor
sailing	manhood	looker	sorted	mohair
candor	beyond	tenant	table	onus
ailing	under	toga	rotund	magic

f   _____

l   _____

h   _____

y   _____

t   _____

n   _____

k   _____

g   _____

b   _____

d   _____

WORD ATTACK   **A. Knows Consonant Sounds**   4. *Medial sounds*

DIRECTIONS: From the following lists, find three words that have the medial consonant indicated in the left column. Write these words on the line opposite that consonant.

dicker	cohere	saber	deeded	silly
solar	subway	surfing	cinder	cartoon
spangle	dryad	prayer	continue	scapegoat
enhance	rebel	tenure	polar	reduce
befoul	before	darken	beaker	cogent
joyous	exhale	connive	detect	renew

b _____

d _____

g _____

k _____

n _____

t _____

y _____

h _____

l _____

f _____

WORD ATTACK   A. Knows Consonant Sounds   4. *Medial sounds*

DIRECTIONS: From the following lists, find three words that have the medial consonant indicated in the left column. Write these words on the line opposite that consonant.

breakage	lawyer	lunar	leafy	behead
timber	color	static	anew	unholy
dandy	leakage	dryer	carding	digital
below	bauble	satire	surfeit	tango
tonic	rugged	infect	party	inhibit
cable	bailiff	render	drinker	rayon

d _____

g _____

k _____

n _____

t _____

y _____

h _____

l _____

f _____

b _____

WORD ATTACK   **A. Knows Consonant Sounds**   **5.** *Final sounds*

DIRECTIONS: Read the list of words carefully. Underline only the final consonant sound in the word. If the word does not end with a consonant sound, do not make any marks.

1. desk   11. shining

2. cross   12. dell

3. flapper   13. discern

4. lax   14. phonics

5. fellow   15. fate

6. toe   16. gap

7. things   17. song

8. fluke   18. lot

9. fault   19. early

10. finite   20. brim

WORD ATTACK   A. Knows Consonant Sounds   5. _Final sounds_

DIRECTIONS: Read the list of words carefully. Underline only the final consonant sound in the word. If the word does not end with a consonant sound, do not make any mark.

1. music

2. concern

3. map

4. sings

5. long

6. sad

7. mass

8. malt

9. lag

10. duke

11. brake

12. doe

13. lining

14. dread

15. refute

16. pot

17. safe

18. knell

19. lyrics

20. dryer

WORD ATTACK   A. Knows Consonant Sounds   5. *Final sounds*

DIRECTIONS: Read the list of words carefully. Underline only the final consonant sound in the word. If the word does not end with a consonant sound, do not make any mark.

1. fell

2. prongs

3. lass

4. critics

5. loser

6. like

7. default

8. urn

9. tax

10. surly

11. fox

12. cite

13. scream

14. not

15. sagging

16. fern

17. sap

18. gong

19. break

20. lull

WORD ATTACK   **A. Knows Consonant Sounds**   **5. *Final sounds***

DIRECTIONS: Read the list of words carefully. Underline only the final consonant sound in the word. If the word does not end with a consonant sound, do not make any mark.

1. fighter	11. soft
2. pell-mell	12. nagging
3. thongs	13. physics
4. fin	14. earn
5. foe	15. dot
6. grim	16. mute
7. sick	17. dike
8. bong	18. dreaming
9. easy	19. lap
10. grass	20. pull

WORD ATTACK   **B. Hears and Can Make Vowel Sounds   1.** *Long vowels*
Short vowels

DIRECTIONS: Read the words in the left column carefully. Then, place a breve (⌣) over the short vowel sounds and a macron (—) over the long vowel sounds. Next, look at the words in the right column. Write each word phonetically, using the breve or macron where needed.

	sweat	(swĕt)
Example: kīnd	*Example:* bow	(bō)
pĭg		
rōpe	nose	(nōz)

1. pain   11. deaf   (_____)

2. she   12. post   (_____)

3. left   13. coat   (_____)

4. pin   14. line   (_____)

5. fun   15. rib   (_____)

6. loon   16. mole   (_____)

7. fight   17. move   (_____)

8. mid   18. oasis   (_____)

9. frame   19. mow   (_____)

10. frill   20. money   (_____)

WORD ATTACK   **B. Hears and Can Make Vowel Sounds**   **1.** *Long vowels*
Short vowels

DIRECTIONS: Read the words in the left column carefully. Then, place a breve (◡) over the short vowel sounds and a macron (—) over the long vowel sounds. Next, look at the words in the right column. Write each word phonetically, using the breve or macron where needed.

k̄ind   sweat   (sw̆et)
Example: p̆ig   *Example:* bow   (bō)
r̄ope   nose   (nōz)

1. feet   11. sow   (_____)

2. let   12. tune   (_____)

3. cold   13. post   (_____)

4. raid   14. map   (_____)

5. lens   15. nape   (_____)

6. mow   16. poke   (_____)

7. mode   17. mew   (_____)

8. moon   18. groove   (_____)

9. seat   19. like   (_____)

10. hope   20. none   (_____)

WORD ATTACK   B. Hears and Can Make Vowel Sounds   1. *Long vowels*
                                                        Short vowels

DIRECTIONS: Read the words in the left column carefully. Then, place a breve (⌣) over the short vowel sounds and a macron (—) over the long vowel sounds. Next, look at the words in the right column. Write each word phonetically, using the breve or macron where needed.

	k͞ind	sweat	(sw⌣et)
Example:	p⌣ig	*Example:* bow	(b͞o)
	r͞ope	nose	(n͞oz)

1. low	11. mope	(_____)
2. ore	12. oar	(_____)
3. rake	13. gad	(_____)
4. lime	14. peck	(_____)
5. geld	15. leach	(_____)
6. wreck	16. mule	(_____)
7. moot	17. pea	(_____)
8. fear	18. gear	(_____)
9. pun	19. hip	(_____)
10. grit	20. game	(_____)

Name: _____   Date: _____

DIRECTIONS: Read the words in the left column carefully. Then, place a breve (‿) over the short vowel sounds and a macron (—) over the long vowel sounds. Next, look at the words in the right column. Write each word phonetically, using the breve or macron where needed.

k͞ind   sweat   (swĕet)

Example: pĭg   *Example:* bow   (bō)

r͞ope   nose   (nōz)

1. lap   11. nude   (_____)

2. plum   12. four   (_____)

3. fickle   13. gay   (_____)

4. boon   14. ace   (_____)

5. feat   15. golf   (_____)

6. gold   16. hobo   (_____)

7. peach   17. feed   (_____)

8. us   18. moon   (_____)

9. lame   19. joke   (_____)

10. meet   20. muck   (_____)

WORD ATTACK   **B. Hears and Can Make Vowel Sounds**   **2. *Can apply vowel rules***

DIRECTIONS: Read the vowel rule. Then, mark the sound of the vowels in the words that follow it, long vowel (—), short vowel (‿), or silent vowel (/).

A. A single vowel at the beginning or in the middle of a one-syllable word is usually short.

     1. ask   3. bed   5. is   7. egg   9. nod

     2. pad   4. odd   6. doll   8. sill   10. us

B. A single vowel at the end of a one-syllable word is usually long.

     1. Ho!   2. me   3. we   4. no   5. Hi!

C. When two vowels are together in a one-syllable word, the first vowel is usually long and the second is silent.

     1. lease   3. due   5. bait   7. foam   9. pie

     2. coat   4. goal   6. meat   8. near   10. rue

D. When there are two vowels in a one-syllable word and one is a final *e*, the first is usually long and the second is silent.

     1. mate   3. ruse   5. rote   7. tole   9. nape

     2. nine   4. vale   6. brute   8. game   10. cone

E. A vowel followed by *rr* is usually short.

     1. embarrass   3. furrow   5. serrate

     2. irrigate   4. surrey

WORD ATTACK   **B. Hears and Can Make Vowel Sounds**   **2. *Can apply vowel rules***

DIRECTIONS: Read the vowel rule. Then, mark the sound of the vowels in the words that follow it, long vowel (—), short vowel (⌣), or silent vowel (/).

A. A single vowel at the beginning or in the middle of a one-syllable word is usually short.

1. etch	3. add	5. lad	7. bin	9. rut
2. ill	4. on	6. pond	8. up	10. hem

B. A single vowel at the end of a one-syllable word is usually long.

1. by	2. go	3. he	4. a	5. so

C. When two vowels are together in a one-syllable word, the first vowel is usually long and the second is silent.

1. shoal	3. feat	5. boat	7. fail	9. lie
2. rain	4. cue	6. cease	8. least	10. due

D. When there are two vowels in a one-syllable word and one is a final *e*, the first is usually long and the second is silent.

1. late	3. fuse	5. dope	7. cope	9. bone
2. fine	4. sale	6. lute	8. same	10. pose

E. A vowel followed by *rr* is usually short.

1. squirrel	3. furry	5. mirror
2. borrow	4. derrick	

WORD ATTACK   **B. Hears and Can Make Vowel Sounds**   2. *Can apply vowel rules*

DIRECTIONS: Read the vowel rule. Then, mark the sound of the vowels in the words that follow it, long vowel (—), short vowel (‿), or silent vowel (/).

A. A single vowel at the beginning or in the middle of a one-syllable word is usually short.

1. am	3. ebb	5. lit	7. lush	9. opt
2. pond	4. if	6. lack	8. bet	10. fin

B. A single vowel at the end of a one-syllable word is usually long.

1. so	2. shy	3. do (in music)	4. lo!	5. pi (in math)

C. When two vowels are together in a one-syllable word, the first vowel is usually long and the second is silent.

1. die	3. lead	5. moan	7. bail	9. feast
2. gloat	4. tie	6. glue	8. foal	10. ear

D. When there are two vowels in a one-syllable word and one is a final *e*, the first is usually long and the second is silent.

1. date	3. mire	5. cute	7. page	9. lone
2. time	4. pope	6. rose	8. pale	10. those

E. A vowel followed by *rr* is usually short.

1. err	3. barrel	5. ferret
2. irregular	4. quarrel	

WORD ATTACK   B. Hears and Can Make Vowel Sounds   2. *Can apply vowel rules*

DIRECTIONS: Read the vowel rule. Then, mark the sound of the vowels in the words that follow it, long vowel (—), short vowel (⌣), or silent vowel (/).

A. A single vowel at the beginning or in the middle of a one-syllable word is usually short.

1. but	3. pack	5. debt	7. elf	9. sin
2. luck	4. pot	6. in	8. oft	10. an

B. A single vowel at the end of a one-syllable word is usually long.

1. ye	2. cry	3. dry	4. she	5. be

C. When two vowels are together in a one-syllable word, the first vowel is usually long and the second is silent.

1. reed	3. moat	5. beast	7. fie!	9. roan
2. hue	4. beak	6. toast	8. woe	10. mail

D. When there are two vowels in a one-syllable word and one is a final *e*, the first is usually long and the second is silent.

1. cope	3. gate	5. gale	7. wage	9. use
2. note	4. wine	6. doze	8. dame	10. hope

E. A vowel followed by *rr* is usually short.

1. error	2. hurry	3. merry	4. sorrel	5. parry

WORD ATTACK   C. Knows Elements of Syllabication   1. *Knows rules*

DIRECTIONS: Each group of words illustrates one of the rules of syllabication. Write the letter that heads the group opposite the rule it illustrates.

a.	b.	c.	d.	e.
po ta to	arm ful	spar row	pre judge	fa tal
ta ble	dis arm	ser mon	ab normal	em ber
re cess	arm let	fer ment	in sane	in
mo bile	arm hole	mer cy	non sense	ge ni us

f.	g.	h.	i.	j.
u ku le le	man hood	sen si ble	se cret	col lect
a men	poor ly	fid dle	re frain	par son
o dor	per il ous	mul ti ple	en grave	fac tor
i rate	state ment	star tle	in flate	im por tant

_____ 1. Each syllable must have a vowel.

_____ 2. A single vowel can be a syllable.

_____ 3. Prefixes are syllables.

_____ 4. Suffixes are syllables.

_____ 5. Root words are syllables and are not divided.

_____ 6. If a vowel in a syllable is followed by two consonants, the syllable ends with the first consonant.

_____ 7. If a vowel in a syllable is followed by only one consonant, the syllable ends with the vowel.

_____ 8. If a word ends in *le*, the consonant just before the *l* begins the last syllable.

_____ 9. When there is an *r* after a vowel, the *r* goes with the vowel.

_____ 10. Consonant blends are not divided.

WORD ATTACK   C. Knows Elements of Syllabication   1. *Knows rules*

DIRECTIONS: Each group of words illustrates one of the rules of syllabication. Write the letter that heads the group opposite the rule it illustrates.

a.	b.	c.	d.	e.
u ni fy	girl hood	gar lic	har ass	a head
a do	like ly	he ro	car a mel	fore head
o boe	dan ger ous	tur key	par lor	head ed
e go	ac tiv ist	is land	bor ing	head ing

f.	g.	h.	i.	j.
ca pa ble	re try	mo tel	cour te sy	im pa tience
i ci cle	whisk er	su per	mer ci ful	in tan gi ble
sub tle	sym pa thy	ste ve dore	fel low	dis charge
bub ble	mid ship man	re lay	cor rect	pre test

_____ 1. Each syllable must have a vowel.

_____ 2. A single vowel can be a syllable.

_____ 3. Prefixes are syllables.

_____ 4. Suffixes are syllables.

_____ 5. Root words are syllables and are not divided.

_____ 6. If a vowel in a syllable is followed by two consonants, the syllable ends with the first consonant.

_____ 7. If a vowel in a syllable is followed by only one consonant, the syllable ends with the vowel.

_____ 8. If a word ends in *le*, the consonant just before the *l* begins the last syllable.

_____ 9. When there is an *r* after a vowel, the *r* goes with the vowel.

_____ 10. Consonant blends are not divided.

WORD ATTACK   C. Knows Elements of Syllabication   1. *Knows rules*

DIRECTIONS: Each group of words illustrates one of the rules of syllabication. Write the letter that heads the group opposite the rule it illustrates.

a.	b.	c.	d.	e.
pro noun	au di ble	quo rum	vow el	i de a
trans port	au di ence	be gan	sin gle	a gree
de pose	good ness	au di o	a go	o nus
un real	bold ness	re gal	to	e ject

f.	g.	h.	i.	j.
grass y	ta ble	sit ting	spar ing	slip shod
late ly	rid dle	strug gle	har bor	ski er
sharp ness	gig gle	crum ple	car a van	pa tri ot
dis band	fiz zle	pre dic tion	gar ish	tri umph

_____ 1. Each syllable must have a vowel.

_____ 2. A single vowel can be a syllable.

_____ 3. Prefixes are syllables.

_____ 4. Suffixes are syllables.

_____ 5. Root words are syllables and are not divided.

_____ 6. If a vowel in a syllable is followed by two consonants, the syllable ends with the first consonant.

_____ 7. If a vowel in a syllable is followed by only one consonant, the syllable ends with the vowel.

_____ 8. If a word ends in *le*, the consonant just before the *l* begins the last syllable.

_____ 9. When there is an *r* after a vowel, the *r* goes with the vowel.

_____ 10. Consonant blends are not divided.

WORD ATTACK   **C. Knows Elements of Syllabication**   **1. *Knows rules***

DIRECTIONS: Each pair of words illustrates one of the rules of syllabication. Write the letter that heads the pair in the space next to the rule it illustrates.

a.	b.	c.	d.	e.
fer vor	i dle	ar ti cle	at tic	di vine
ger und	o pen	prob a ble	di vid ed	pa per

f.	g.	h.	i.	j.
in flu ence	con so nant	sub way	up heav al	rest ive
in grate	dis mal	un sound	re tread	pain less

_____ 1. Each syllable must have a vowel.

_____ 2. A single vowel can be a syllable.

_____ 3. Prefixes are syllables.

_____ 4. Suffixes are syllables.

_____ 5. Root words are syllables and are not divided.

_____ 6. If a vowel in a syllable is followed by two consonants, the syllable ends with the first consonant.

_____ 7. If a vowel in a syllable is followed by only one consonant, the syllable ends with the vowel.

_____ 8. If a word ends in *le*, the consonant just before the *l* begins the last syllable.

_____ 9. When there is an *r* after a vowel, the *r* goes with the vowel.

_____ 10. Consonant blends are not divided.

WORD ATTACK   **C. Knows Elements of Syllabication**   **2. *Can apply rules***

DIRECTIONS: Divide the words that follow into syllables by making a slash mark (/) between the appropriate letters.

A.

1. e t h e r
2. s e c e d e
3. p a s s i v e
4. p a r e n t
5. f o l l i c l e

6. t r a n s f e r e n c e
7. s e t t e e
8. l y r i c
9. i m p a i r m e n t
10. u s u r p

B.

11. a m a s s
12. p e r f o r m
13. c a r a v e l
14. r a f f l e
15. d e f e r r a l

16. e f f o r t
17. b e l o w
18. r e f e r
19. e m b l e m
20. g e n i u s

C.

21. h a m m e r
22. a b i d e
23. e c l i p s e
24. t r i p a r t i t e
25. o n l y

26. m y r t l e
27. p e c a n
28. f o r t i f y
29. p u b l i c
30. r u n n i n g

WORD ATTACK   C. Knows Elements of Syllabication   2. *Can apply rules*

DIRECTIONS: Divide the words that follow into syllables by making a slash mark (/) between the appropriate letters.

    1.   p u r v e y

    2.   i o d i n e

    3.   s e r i o u s

    4.   l e a d e r s h i p

    5.   r e c e s s i o n

    6.   m e m b e r s h i p

    7.   s i z z l e

    8.   p a r a b l e

    9.   p a m p h l e t

   10.   m i r a g e

   11.   o p i a t e

   12.   c o e x i s t

DIRECTIONS: Divide the words that follow into syllables by making a slash mark (/) between the appropriate letters.

1. i n f e r e n c e

2. k e y n o t e

3. h u s b a n d

4. h a l y a r d

5. e m o t i o n

6. d i s t a n t

7. c o n v e n t i o n

8. c a d a v e r

9. a n t i b o d y

10. g e n t i l e

11. i n s i d e

12. l e a r n i n g

13. j a n g l e

14. p r e v e n t

WORD ATTACK   **C. Knows Elements of Syllabication**   **2. *Can apply rules***

DIRECTIONS: Divide the words that follow into syllables by making a slash mark (/) between the appropriate letters.

1. k e n n e l

2. h u r t l e

3. h a l l u c i n a t e

4. e m p l o y e r

5. e m e r g e n t

6. d i s t i l l

7. c o n t r a r y

8. b e s p e a k

9. a n c h o r

10. g e n u s

11. i l l u m i n a t e

12. r e s i d e n t

13. s h a k e r

14. s p e c t r u m

15. l e a k a g e

WORD ATTACK   D. Uses Accent Properly   1. *Knows and applies rules*

DIRECTIONS:
1. Divide the words below into syllables, using a slash mark (/).
2. Insert the accent mark (') at the end of the syllable that is stressed.
3. In the space provided, write the letter of the rule below that calls for the accentuation of that syllable.

1. _____ m a n n e r l e s s   11. _____ e m b o l d e n
2. _____ b e m o a n   12. _____ r e v i e w
3. _____ e n t i t l e   13. _____ p r e s e r v e
4. _____ n o m i n a t e   14. _____ i n c e n t i v e
5. _____ e r a s e r   15. _____ d u a l i t y
6. _____ e a t a b l e   16. _____ b e t t e r
7. _____ d e c o y   17. _____ m a n n e r i s m
8. _____ a g r e e   18. _____ a k i n
9. _____ j u s t i f y   19. _____ o r a t o r
10. _____ d e f e n d   20. _____ r e n t a l

a. Beginning syllables *de, re, in, be, er,* and *a* are usually not accented.

b. In a word of two or more syllables, the first syllable is usually accented unless it is a prefix.

c. In most two-syllable words that end in a consonant followed by *y*, the first syllable is accented and the last is unaccented.

d. When a suffix is added, the accent falls on or within the root word.

e. Endings that form syllables are usually unaccented.

f. When a syllable ends in *le*, that syllable is usually unaccented.

WORD ATTACK   D. Uses Accent Properly   1. *Knows and applies rules*

DIRECTIONS:
1. Divide the words below into syllables, using a slash mark (/).
2. Insert the accent mark (') at the end of the syllable that is stressed.
3. In the space provided, write the letter of the rule below that calls for the accentuation of that syllable.

1. _____ d e c e a s e
2. _____ b o u n t i f u l
3. _____ i n c r e a s e
4. _____ p r o m i s e
5. _____ e x p l a i n
6. _____ d a i s y
7. _____ b e t t e r m e n t
8. _____ p r o p e l
9. _____ s e n a t e
10. _____ n a t i o n a l

11. _____ f r a g i l e
12. _____ o n l y
13. _____ b u s y
14. _____ p u l p i t
15. _____ g u i l t y
16. _____ f a t h e r h o o d
17. _____ p r e v e n t
18. _____ c a n d i d
19. _____ s e n s i b l e
20. _____ c h r o n i c l e

a. Beginning syllables *de, re, in, be, er,* and *a* are usually not accented.

b. In a word of two or more syllables, the first syllable is usually accented unless it is a prefix.

c. In most two-syllable words that end in a consonant followed by *y*, the first syllable is accented and the last is unaccented.

d. When a suffix is added, the accent falls on or within the root word.

e. Endings that form syllables are usually unaccented.

f. When a syllable ends in *le*, that syllable is usually unaccented.

Name: _____ Date: _____

WORD ATTACK   D. Uses Accent Properly   1. *Knows and applies rules*

DIRECTIONS:
1. Divide the words below into syllables, using a slash mark (/).
2. Insert the accent mark (') at the end of the syllable that is stressed.
3. In the space provided, write the letter of the rule below that calls for the accentuation of that syllable.

1. _____ p u n c t u r e   11. _____ o r a n g e
2. _____ m o o d y   12. _____ e m e r g e n c y
3. _____ o r a c l e   13. _____ b e q u e s t
4. _____ r e d e e m   14. _____ a b o u t
5. _____ m e d i a t e   15. _____ e r u p t i o n
6. _____ d e c e i v e   16. _____ i d e a l i z e
7. _____ n a u t i c a l   17. _____ o b j e c t
8. _____ c a n d y   18. _____ o r i o l e
9. _____ o g l e   19. _____ o p a l
10. _____ p r e p a y   20. _____ d e m e a n

a. Beginning syllables *de*, *re*, *in*, *be*, *er*, and *a* are usually not accented.

b. In a word of two or more syllables, the first syllable is usually accented unless it is a prefix.

c. In most two-syllable words that end in a consonant followed by *y*, the first syllable is accented and the last is unaccented.

d. When a suffix is added, the accent falls on or within the root word.

e. Endings that form syllables are usually unaccented.

f. When a syllable ends in *le*, that syllable is usually unaccented.

Name: _____ Date: _____

DIRECTIONS:
1. Divide the words below into syllables, using a slash mark (/).
2. Insert the accent mark (') at the end of the syllable that is stressed.

1. e r e c t

2. b e l i e v e

3. a p a r t

4. p u n y

5. r e c e n t

6. u n c u t

7. i n s t a l l m e n t

8. h a b i t a b l e

9. j u s t i f y

10. i n c r e d i b l e

11. r e f i n e

12. o r a c l e

13. s y l l a b l e

14. t r i f l e

15. s e l l e r

16. s u b s i s t

17. c o o p t

18. g a l l a n t r y

19. e d i t o r

20. f a s h i o n

21. p r e s i d e

22. r e q u e s t

23. i n c i d e n t

24. e x i s t

25. s e c e d e

26. s i g n a l

27. c i r c l e

28. c a r r y

29. l u m b e r m a n

30. i c i c l e

31. d e r i v e

32. l a z y

33. s c h e d u l e

34. i n v e n t

35. l i t t l e

36. u n s c r a m b l e

37. j e a l o u s y

38. b e a t a b l e

39. e a s t e r l y

40. a m e n d

WORD ATTACK   D. Uses Accent Properly   2. *Can shift accent and change use of word*

DIRECTIONS: In each of the following sentences, divide the underlined word into syllables, using a slash mark (/). Then, insert an accent mark (') to show the syllable needing stress because of the use of the word in the sentence.

1. Prince Albert was the c o n s o r t of Queen Victoria.

2. To c o n s o r t with friends of questionable character is not likely to result in being influenced for the better.

3. Packaging is done so successfully that the c o n t e n t of a parcel, even if fragile, arrives intact.

4. Will she be c o n t e n t to remain in a small college town after spending a year with Paris as her campus?

5. The workers' c o n t r a c t is due to expire at midnight.

6. We will c o n t r a c t with a plumber to make the necessary repairs.

7. The lieutenant was reprimanded for c o n d u c t unbecoming an officer and a gentleman.

8. Because of a broken arm, the maestro will not c o n d u c t the symphony this evening.

9. Carefully, his father put the letter back in the e n v e l o p e.

10. The fog will e n v e l o p you and you will be lost.

WORD ATTACK   D. Uses Accent Properly   2. *Can shift accent and change use of word*

DIRECTIONS: In each of the following sentences, divide the underlined word into syllables, using a slash mark (/). Then, insert an accent mark (') to show the syllable needing stress because of the use of the word in the sentence.

1. Without the c o m b i n e, harvesting grain would take much longer.

2. If you c o m b i n e effort and hard work with good intentions, you will know success.

3. If you are going to be a r e b e l, be one with a good cause.

4. R e b e l if you must, but be sure you know the possible consequences and are ready to accept them.

5. Marion's p r o g r e s s with her music has simply been unprecedented.

6. We will p r o g r e s s slowly to make sure you understand each step of the operation as we go along.

7. Have you ever tried to p r o j e c t numbers for the future?

8. The p r o j e c t was turned down for apparently no good reason.

9. Have you learned to c o n v e r t a fraction to a decimal?

10. He is a c o n v e r t from polytheism to monotheism.

Name: _____ Date: _____

WORD ATTACK   D. Uses Accent Properly   2. *Can shift accent and*
                                             change use of word

DIRECTIONS: In each of the following sentences, divide the underlined word into syllables, using a slash mark (/). Then, insert an accent mark (') to show the syllable needing stress because of the use of the word in the sentence.

1. The loser decided not to c o n t e s t the results of the election.

2. There really was no c o n t e s t between the two fighters.

3. Many Olympic champions have broken r e c o r d s.

4. History will not favorably r e c o r d lack of efforts for peacemaking.

5. Peter and Frances decided to c o n v e r s e quietly.

6. If a statement is true, its c o n v e r s e may not be true.

7. Will the jury c o n v i c t the person on trial?

8. People object to having prisons located near their homes because they do not want c o n v i c t s in their neighborhood.

9. The temperature of forty degrees this morning was in sharp c o n t r a s t to yesterday's eighty degrees.

10. C o n t r a s t the characters of the hero and the villain.

WORD ATTACK   D. Uses Accent Properly   2. *Can shift accent and*
                                              change use of word

DIRECTIONS: In each of the following sentences, divide the underlined word into syllables. using a slash mark (/). Then, insert an accent mark (') to show the syllable needing stress because of the way the word is used in the sentence.

1. To c o n s c r i p t is to draft for military or naval service.

2. A recruit obtained through conscription is called a c o n s c r i p t.

3. Try as she might, their mother was unable to c o n s o l e them for their loss.

4. At the c o n s o l e of the organ sat the greatest organ player of the day.

5. We were able to get really fresh p r o d u c e at the local farmers' market.

6. The graduating class will p r o d u c e a play that one of its members composed.

7. The coach was c o n f i d e n t that his team would win.

8. Formerly, rulers had c o n f i d a n t s; nowadays, they have advisers.

9. The aircraft carrier was not part of the c o n v o y.

10. Three fighter planes will c o n v o y the president's plane.

COMPREHENSION **A. Understands Structure of Story 1.** *Main idea*
or Paragraph **2.** *Topic sentence*
3. *Sequence of ideas*
4. *Subordinate ideas*

DIRECTIONS: As you read the following selection, look for (1) the main idea, (2) the topic sentence, (3) the sequence of ideas, and (4) subordinate ideas. For item number 1 below, check (✓) the statement that best describes the main idea of the passage. For items 2, 3, and 4, write the sentence numbers in the spaces provided to indicate your answer.

[1]Four principal land regions make up the state of Missouri. [2]Their designations bring to the mind's eye wide, flat expanses. [3]North of the Missouri River are the Dissected Till Plains; in the west are the Osage Plains; the southeast corner is covered by the West Gulf Coastal Plain, known locally as the Mississippi Alluvial Plain; and the largest region, the southern section, is the Ozark Plateau. [4]The Central Lowlands are subdivided by the Dissected Till and the Osage Plains. [5]In the Ozark region, a major and popular vacationland evolved from the creation of ten major artificial lakes formed by dams. [6]They contribute largely to the state's nearly one billion dollar annual tourism business. [7]While forests formerly covered two-thirds of the state, today they cover only about half of that. [8]This includes the Mark Twain and the Clark National Forests.

1. The best statement of the *main idea* is:

 _____ Missouri is a forest country.

 _____ Missouri is flat country.

 _____ Missouri is vacation country.

2. _____ Write the number of the *topic sentence.*

3. _____ Write the number of each major idea in the passage in the *sequence* in which the ideas were presented.

4. _____ Write the number of each of the *subordinate ideas* presented in the passage.

Name: _____ Date: _____

COMPREHENSION   A. Understands Structure of Story   1. *Main idea*
                     or Paragraph   2. *Topic sentence*
                                                        3. *Sequence of ideas*
                                                        4. *Subordinate ideas*

DIRECTIONS: As you read the following selection, look for (1) the main idea, (2) the topic sentence, (3) the sequence of ideas, and (4) subordinate ideas. For item number 1 below, check (✓) the statement that best describes the main idea of the selection. For items 2, 3, and 4, write the sentence numbers in the spaces provided to indicate your answer.

[1]A solution to the twin problems of rising cost and scarcity of anything is to use it less. [2]In the field of energy conservation, this is widely and almost unanimously recognized as the quickest and least costly way to reduce our dependence on foreign oil. [3]The surest way of using less of anything is "doing without." [4]That means, for example, using an oscillating fan instead of an air conditioner. [5]Doing without is not an unusual predicament in life, but it is seldom an appealing situation. [6]It is not all bad. [7]Another way to conserve is "doing as much, or more, with less." [8]This requires finding more efficient ways of using energy so less is demanded for a task. [9]Insulating a house, for example, can reduce the amount of energy needed to heat it. [10]A less weighty automobile with a differently designed engine can consume less petrol and still transport you. [11]After "doing without" and "doing more with less" are exhausted, however, a plateau is reached. [12]Then other avenues to conserve must be pursued.

1. The best statement of the *main idea* is:
   _____ Rising cost and scarcity are twin problems.
   _____ We must get used to doing things differently.
   _____ Doing without is a means of conservation.

2. _____ Write the number of the *topic sentence*.

3. _____ Write the number of each major idea in the selection. List the numbers in the *sequence* in which the ideas were presented.

4. _____ Write the number of each of the *subordinate ideas* presented in the selection.

COMPREHENSION   **A. Understands Structure of Story or Paragraph**   1. *Main idea*
2. *Topic sentence*
3. *Sequence of ideas*
4. *Subordinate ideas*

DIRECTIONS: As you read the following selection, look for (1) the main idea, (2) the topic sentence, (3) the sequence of ideas, and (4) subordinate ideas. For item number 1 below, check (✓) the statement that best describes the main idea of the selection. For items 2, 3, and 4, write the sentence numbers in the spaces provided to indicate your answer.

[1]An alternative method to picking weeds by hand or killing them with chemicals has been rediscovered. [2]Since the former is very expensive and the latter deemed harmful to soil and crop, the rediscovery is important. [3]The method is using Chinese Weeder geese to weed crops. [4]As their name suggests, the breed originated in China and was first produced some 2000 years ago. [5]With cross-breeding, this type of goose is now about the size of a swan. [6]They can be used to weed many crops. [7]They may, however, nibble at leafy plants such as spinach or lettuce. [8]They cannot be used to weed grain crops but can be used for corn after the plants reach a certain height. [9]Instead of chemical contamination, the soil receives enrichment because goose manure is good fertilizer. [10]Neither is the soil compacted by the geese as it would be by a tractor which would itself need petroleum to operate. [11]While the initial cost is about the same as using chemicals, the geese become cheaper to use.

1. The best statement of the *main idea* is:
   _____ Weeds are picked by hand or killed by chemicals.
   _____ Geese are effective, efficient crop weeders.
   _____ There is an alternative way to weed crops.

2. _____ Write the number of the *topic sentence.*

3. _____ Write the number of each major idea in the selection. List the numbers in the *sequence* in which the ideas were presented.

4. _____ Write the number of each of the *subordinate ideas* presented in the selection.

COMPREHENSION A. **Understands Structure of Story** 1. *Main idea*
or Paragraph 2. *Topic sentence*
3. *Sequence of ideas*
4. *Subordinate ideas*

DIRECTIONS: As you read the following selection, look for (1) the main idea, (2) the topic sentence, (3) the sequence of ideas, and (4) subordinate ideas. For item number 1 below, check (✓) the statement that best describes the main idea of the passage. For items 2, 3, and 4, write the sentence numbers in the spaces provided to indicate your answer.

[1]It would be difficult to overstate the conditions that prevailed at Valley Forge that fateful winter. [2]Ill-clothed, poorly housed, meagerly fed, the Continental Army fell easy victim to disease, fear, discontent, desertion, and death. [3]By February, nearly three thousand men had died of exposure or disease. [4]The Commander-in-Chief himself had narrowly escaped removal at the hands of a conspiracy that had been directed against him. [5]Morale was low despite the troops' fierce loyalty to their general. [6]It was hardly a hopeful scene. [7]Yet, into that now legendary agony came an officer of the Prussian army, drawn, as were other foreigners, by a personal commitment to freedom. [8]Baron Friedrich Wilhelm von Steuben, then 48, had been an officer at 17. [9]He had served as an infantry officer and later as a staff officer. [10]His training was just what Washington's embattled forces sorely needed.

1. The best statement of the *main idea* is:
   _____ Conditions could not have been worse.
   _____ It was a fateful winter.
   _____ There was a conspiracy against the Commander-in-Chief.

2. _____ Write the number of the *topic sentence.*

3. _____ Write the number of each major idea in the selection. List the numbers in the *sequence* in which the ideas were presented.

4. _____ Write the number of each of the *subordinate ideas* presented in the passage.

COMPREHENSION   **B. Can Repeat General Idea of Material Read**
C. Can Remember Specific Important Facts
D. Can Relate Material Read to Known Information or Experience

DIRECTIONS: Read the selection below carefully. Then answer the questions that follow.

Dentists, it would appear, are an endangered species today. They are not as busy as they would like to be nor is their income at the level they would like. No longer is it necessary for patients to wait a long time for an appointment. Some dentists, in fact, are looking for ways to attract patients.

Why should it come as a surprise? You may recall those television advertisements showing children returning from their routine visit to the dentist shouting, "No cavities!" And what about all those claims about what was killing bacteria in the mouth? Well, the *Wall Street Journal* reported recently that improved oral hygiene is a fact. It is having an impact on the demand—or lack of it—for dentists' services.

Another contributor to the current status of the dentist is the success in spreading the practice of fluoridation. The current economic state of recession is also accused of diminishing the need for dentists. Many dental services are considered to be elective and are put off, reducing the demand upon dentists. To compound the situation, the number of dentists entering the profession is increasing just at the time when the demand for dentists' services appears to be decreasing.

It is doubtful that the dentists will let themselves become extinct. Time will reveal what they will undertake to change the situation.

1. Briefly state the general idea of the passage. _____

_____

2. Give four specific facts: _____

_____

_____

3. Using past experience and information, answer the following questions:

   a. Was the toothpaste and mouthwash advertising successful? _____

   How? _____

   b. How do dentists feel about the situation? _____

   _____

   c. Will dentists be satisfied to leave things as they are? _____

_____

Name: _____ Date: _____

B. Can Repeat General Idea of Material Read
C. Can Remember Specific Important Facts
D. Can Relate Material Read to Known Information or Experience

DIRECTIONS: Read the selection below carefully. Then answer the questions that follow.

It is almost a rule of thumb that there are as many house rats as there are people. Health officials fear that we may soon be outnumbered by them. Because they can spread diseases such as typhus, tylaremia, and rabies, they are enemies.

Why are they so numerous? Rats generally live where there are people because that guarantees them an abundant supply of food. They will eat anything. They are aggressive, intelligent, and adaptable. They multiply extremely fast. All of these traits enable them to outsmart the people who wage war against them.

Not only are they attracted by garbage, but they will also invade food supplies using their long, pointed muzzles and dexterous forepaws. They burrow easily and only very small holes are needed for them to gain entrance.

Rats are extremely fecund. Females produce as many as eight litters a year with as many as twenty young per litter. It takes only three weeks for a rat to gestate. Some live as long as four years.

How to stop this enemy? Keeping premises clean is the first step in the battle against rats which must be constant and relentless. Storing wood and similar objects away from walls will deny them places to hide. Rats are cunning, and they soon learn to avoid traps which in turn become ineffective. Garbage must be made invasion-proof. But even all these measures are insufficient.

A newer measure is to bait them with small bags of food containing an anticoagulant drug. These attract the omnivorous rats, who eat the drugged food and eventually die from internal bleeding.

1. Briefly state the general idea of the passage. _____

_____

2. State five specific, important facts. _____

_____

_____

3. Using past experience and information, answer the following questions:

   a. Why should we wage war on rats? _____

   b. Why are rats difficult to exterminate? _____

   c. Can new measures of extermination be administered by ordinary people? Why?

_____

   d. Can you think of disadvantages to the method? _____

COMPREHENSION   **B. Can Repeat General Idea of Material Read**
C. Can Remember Specific Important Facts
D. Can Relate Material Read to Known Information or Experience

DIRECTIONS: Read the selection below carefully. Then answer the questions that follow.

Our ties with the mother country of England were not severed by the simple act of a declaration of independence, the two-hundredth anniversary of which we celebrated as our nation's birthday in 1976. Some events that resulted from that daring step are still being commemorated.

So it was that on September 28, 1980, two hundred years after the day on which it occurred, the arrest of Major Andre, after his meeting with the traitor Benedict Arnold on the shores of the Hudson River, was dramatized. Not only his arrest, but his subsequent imprisonment, trial, conviction for spying, and execution by hanging were all faithfully re-created. The local historical society's carefully preserved records permitted accurate reproduction of costumes, conversations, speeches, and incidents. Even the young man who portrayed Major Andre bore an uncanny resemblance to pictures of him, thanks to a look-alike contest conducted by the historical society.

School children were the special beneficiaries of the celebration. A page of history came alive in a manner that they will remember vividly. Now they know a compelling reason why old buildings, familiar to them but the very ones in which the circumstances unrolled originally, are preserved as historical monuments.

1. Briefly state the general idea of the passage. _____

_____

2. List at least four important, specific facts. _____

_____

_____

3. Using past experiences and information, answer these questions:

a. How was the re-creation of events possible? _____

_____

b. How will the school children feel about their village after this? _____

_____

c. Why will this be remembered more vividly than by reading about it in a book?

_____

COMPREHENSION **B. Can Repeat General Idea of Material Read**
C. Can Remember Specific Important Facts
D. Can Relate Material Read to Known Information and Experience

DIRECTIONS: Read the selection below. Then answer the questions.

Sesame Place is not part of a television show. Neither is it a neighborhood playground. Would you accept a new concept in family entertainment? This first of a new breed is now open in Pennsylvania. There are plans for others to spring up around the country and even throughout the world. They will all operate on the belief that a child's physical and mental energy combined with adult ingenuity can come up with more excitement than a roller coaster ride. The stress is on taking part, putting hands on, rather than merely observing.

Sesame Place has acres and acres with really new and different outdoor activities in Land, Air, and Water Courts. In each of these, children of varying ages will have the opportunity to play and experiment with these elements according to their own level of development and ability. For indoor fun, there is a Science and Games Pavilion. Here are setups to create and illustrate stories by computer, operate miniature industrial plants using remote mechanical hands, and other similarly exciting adventures.

The approach is educational throughout, even in the restaurant where various dishes can be observed being prepared from scratch. Learning and having fun doing it is what it is all about.

The complex is a brainchild of the Children's Television Workshop, creators of "Sesame Street," "The Electric Company," and Busch Gardens, who operate theme parks in Williamsburg, Virginia, and Tampa, Florida.

1. Briefly state the general idea of the passage. _____

_____

2. List at least four specific, important facts. _____

_____

_____

3. Using past experiences and information, answer these questions:

   a. Is this place, with its "hands on" policy, likely to work? _____

   Why? _____

   b. How do you react to reading about Sesame Place? _____

_____

COMPREHENSION   **E. Can Follow Printed Directions**

DIRECTIONS: Read the following directions and record your responses below each one.

1. Write the following words in three equal columns alphabetically: jingle, satisfy, material, yesterday, meal, unless, begin, eventual, outcome, last, pencil, book.

2. Print the vowels of the alphabet.

3. Write your full name: first name, middle name(s), last name.

4. Place your pencil point at the dot marked A. From there, draw a downward curve to B and a right outward curve to C. Continue an outward left curve to D and end it at A. Connect C to B with a left curve.

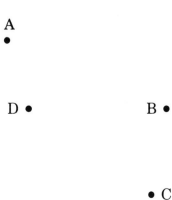

COMPREHENSION   E. Can Follow Printed Directions

DIRECTIONS: Read the directions for each of the items below and then record your responses for each one.

1. Using a ruler, draw parallel lines from A to B and then from C to D.

    A •   • B

    C •   • D

2. Write your teacher's name in this order: title (Mr., Mrs., Miss, Ms., Dr.), first name, middle initial (if there is one), last name.

3. Print the full name of the President of the United States.

4. Place the point of your pencil or pen on the dot marked A. From there, draw a curve downward from A to the dot at B, then another curve under from B upward to A, a straight line down from A to C, a downward curve from C to D, then from D to B to E to F and then back to B.

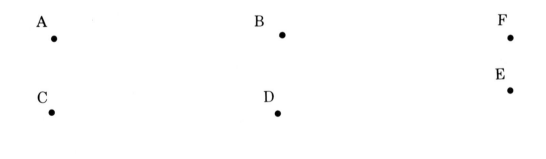

© 1996 by The Center for Applied Research in Education, Inc.

COMPREHENSION   E. Can Follow Printed Directions

DIRECTIONS: Read the directions for each of the items below and then record your responses for each one.

1. Print the name of the governor of your state in capital letters.

2. Write the numbers from 12 to 26, exclusively, in groups of threes, separating each number in a group by a comma and each group by a hyphen.

3. Of the following words, write those that follow the order of the vowels **a**, **e**, **i**, **o**, **u**: jam, money, instantaneous, foolish, ambivalence, grate, cheese, excellence, unsatisfactory, frustration, outrage, quackery.

4. Sign your name with a flourish.

COMPREHENSION   E. Can Follow Printed Directions

DIRECTIONS: Read the directions for each of the items below and then record your responses.

1. In capital letters, print the letters of the alphabet that come immediately after each of the vowels. Then, in small or lower-case letters, print the last five letters of the alphabet.

2. Write the word *excellent* five times, beginning with letters just about as high as these, then each word in letters higher than the previous one.

3. Place the point of your pencil at the dot at M. Draw a line to L; from there go to 2, up to K, and right to 3; go up from there to H, out to G, up to 6, and out to F; continue up to E, down to 5, and in to C; down again to 1, in to A, and down to D; go right from D to 7, down to B, left to 4, down to N, and finish at M. What do you have?

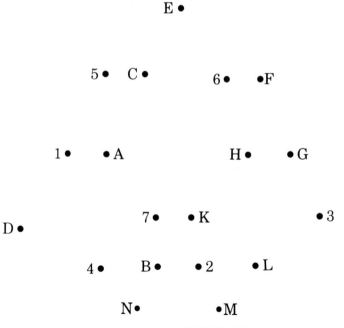

© 1996 by The Center for Applied Research in Education, Inc.

COMPREHENSION   F. Can Interpret Hidden Meaning

DIRECTIONS: Read the following statements. Decide what the hidden meaning is in each one and explain that hidden meaning in the space below.

1. Unless you vote for me, there will be widespread unemployment.

2. The closing of the Drof Plant is a knockout blow to our community.

3. You say your car gets 20 miles per gallon in city traffic? Why be satisfied with that? Buy one of our new models.

4. Weather permitting, we will go skiing this weekend.

5. The picture on the magazine cover will appeal to dog lovers.

COMPREHENSION   **F. Can Interpret Hidden Meaning**

DIRECTIONS: Read the following passages. Decide what the hidden meaning is in each one, if any. Explain the hidden meaning in the space provided.

1. They laughed at him when he started that strange business. Now he's laughing all the way to the bank.

2. All the gold in China could not persuade her to travel by airplane.

3. Just you wait until my ship comes in!

4. She is a knockout!

5. Pack up your troubles!

COMPREHENSION   **F. Can Interpret Hidden Meaning**

DIRECTIONS: Read the following passages. Decide what the hidden meaning is in each one, if any. Explain the hidden meaning in the space provided.

1. Don't trouble trouble until trouble troubles you.

2. The farmer's fields are parched and cracked. Even the leaves on the trees are drooping.

3. A John D. Rockefeller he isn't.

4. When it comes to public speaking, he just isn't a Dr. Martin Luther King.

5. Don't put all your eggs in one basket.

COMPREHENSION   **F. Can Interpret Hidden Meaning**

DIRECTIONS: Read the following statements. Decide what the hidden meaning is in each one, if any. Explain the hidden meaning in the space provided.

1. The end of Abraham Lincoln's famous Gettysburg Address was greeted by a long silence which finally gave way to applause.

2. The classroom windows are open to a warm, sun-filled autumn day. Gradually, the quiet is broken by a trickle of children's voices. The trickle becomes a flood and there is finally a loud, happy, undistinguishable babble of voices.

3. The students were half out of their seats or completely so. Some were standing, some whispering, shoving, and giggling. Suddenly, as if someone had pressed a button, it stopped.

4. Mind your p's and q's.

5. They laughed when the clown sat at the piano and announced he would play *Rhapsody in Blue*. Wild applause replaced the quiet when he finished.

COMPREHENSION A. Interpretation *1. Sequences events from multiple sources*
2. Makes generalizations from multiple sources
3. Identifies relationships of elements from multiple sources

DIRECTIONS: Complete the following, using the information provided.

a. Rivers rising over their banks, flooding
b. A winter with many heavy snowfalls
c. People homeless, heavy water damage
d. Sudden, rapid thawing with heavy rainfall

1. Put these four events in the order in which they happened, using the letters that precede them.

   _____   _____   _____   _____

2. Make a general statement in less than ten words about these events.

   _____

   _____

3. How are all of these events related?

   _____

   _____

   _____

COMPREHENSION   **A. Interpretation**   1. *Sequences events from multiple sources*
2. *Makes generalizations from multiple sources*
3. *Identifies relationships of elements from multiple sources*

DIRECTIONS: Complete the following, using the information provided.

    a. 1925 Sears Catalog picture of an electric washing machine and wringer
    b. Picture from an encyclopedia of women beating clothes on rocks by a stream
    c. Scrub board and wooden tub in an antique shop
    d. TV advertisement for an automatic washer and dryer
    e. Picture in a family album of a great uncle pumping a hand-powered washing machine and wringer

1. Put the above five elements in the order in which they happened, using the letters preceding each to identify them.

_____   _____   _____   _____   _____

2. Make a general statement in less than ten words about these events.

_____

_____

3. How are all of these events related?

_____

_____

_____

COMPREHENSION   A. Interpretation   1. *Sequences events from multiple sources*
2. *Makes generalizations from multiple sources*
3. *Identifies relationships of elements from multiple sources*

DIRECTIONS: Complete the following, using the information provided.

   a. From an airplane window, you see a U.S. Postal Service truck backing up to an airplane
   b. In Restored Village, you get a chance to sit in an old stagecoach
   c. History of the Pony Express
   d. In an old magazine, picture of a mailbag hanging from a pole along railroad tracks

1. Put these elements in the order in which they existed, using the letters preceding each to identify them.

   _____   _____   _____   _____

2. Make a general statement in less than ten words about these elements.

   _____

   _____

3. How are all of these elements related?

   _____

   _____

   _____

COMPREHENSION   **A. Interpretation**   1. *Sequences events from multiple sources*
2. *Makes generalizations from multiple sources*
3. *Identifies relationships of elements from multiple sources*

DIRECTIONS: Complete the following, using the information provided.

    a. Kitty Hawk, North Carolina
    b. Goodyear Blimp
    c. Otto Lilienthal's glider flights
    d. *The Spirit of St. Louis*

1. Put these elements in the order in which they came on the scene, using the letters preceding each to identify them.

    _____   _____   _____   _____

2. Make a general statement in less than ten words about these elements.

_____

_____

3. How are all of these elements related?

_____

_____

_____

Name: _____   Date: _____

DIRECTIONS: Explain the author's purpose in writing the following passage.

When decorating your very own first "pad," you can furnish it quickly with inexpensive, poorly built excuses for furniture, all in questionable taste. It will all give out or break down before you do. You might "make do" with contributions and "hand-me-downs" from relatives and friends while you slowly and wisely invest in well-designed, well-constructed pieces, either antique or contemporary, that will last you a lifetime and serve you well.

The author's purpose:

_____

_____

_____

_____

_____

COMPREHENSION   **A. Interpretation**   **4.** *Identifies author's purpose*

DIRECTIONS: Explain the author's purpose in writing the following passage.

When you go through New England to view the trees in their fall splendor, you can drive yourself and catch a sight of the beauty while keeping an eye on the road and watching out for all the other "rubber neckers." But, then, you can also take one of a number of tours given at that time of year. They use special buses built for tourism with windows on the sides and the top of the bus. Relaxing, without a care for the road, you can look ahead, up, on either side, even turn completely around for a different view. You'll get your fill of unforgettable memories of fall's way with nature.

The author's purpose:

_____

_____

_____

_____

_____

COMPREHENSION   A. Interpretation   4. *Identifies author's purpose*

DIRECTIONS: Explain the author's purpose in writing the following passage.

"Just a minute, young man! Where's the fire? What's your hurry? Why are you running?"

"I'm not running!"

"If that's a sample of walking, I'd hate to be around when you are running!"

"I was walking fast. My friends are..."

"You were walking at such a high speed, had you been on a highway you would have been arrested for exceeding the speed limit. You were not looking where you were going; you were bumping into everybody. You came very near to causing me to fall when I stopped you. Don't you realize it's dangerous to run in the halls? You could cause someone to fall. You could fall yourself..."

"I won't fall."

"... and break the only head you have. You've got two arms and two legs so maybe you can afford to break one. But should you fall and hit your head on these terrazzo floors or on the stairs, what then?"

The author's purpose:

_____

_____

_____

_____

_____

COMPREHENSION   A. Interpretation   4. *Identifies author's purpose*

DIRECTIONS: Explain the author's purpose in writing the following passage.

My dear Isabelle,

You asked me for the best route to follow to come here. Route 7 is a good road but it is not a super highway. It meanders lazily through very scenic country, hits a few medium-sized cities, which will have their own local traffic and traffic signals, all of which will slow you down. From where you are, that route will lead you directly into the center of Adamsville. On the other hand, you can take the interstate highway to Munroe, branch off there onto Route 2 for forty miles, and turn off at Route 117 in Adamsville. You'll probably save an hour and the driving will be easier and safer. Didn't you say time was important?
Have a good trip.

Sincerely,
Tillie

The author's purpose:

_____

_____

_____

_____

_____

COMPREHENSION   A. Interpretation   **5.** *Develops use of parts of speech through transformation of sequences*

DIRECTIONS: In each of the following groups of sentences, one sentence communicates the idea in an inconsiderate, harsh way. Identify that sentence and circle the letter that precedes it.

1. a. Such lousy merchandise. Take it back!

   b. I'm returning this merchandise.

   c. Are you trying to pull a fast one?

2. a. You did that wrong.

   b. How can you be so stupid?

   c. Have you ever tried to do it this way?

3. a. You're one hundred percent wrong!

   b. I don't go along with your line of thinking at all.

   c. Are you crazy?

4. a. When brains were given out, you were passed over.

   b. You're just plain stupid!

   c. That isn't exactly the smart thing to do.

5. a. Shut up!

   b. Please don't talk so.

   c. Don't you ever get tired of talking?

COMPREHENSION   **A. Interpretation**   *5. Develops use of parts of speech through transformation of sequences*

DIRECTIONS: In each of the following groups of sentences, one sentence communicates the idea in a gentle, tactful, considerate way. Circle the letter in front of that sentence.

1. a. You call this cleaning?

   b. Oh dear, did you forget to clean the tub?

   c. This is the third time you didn't clean the tub!

2. a. Hey kids, stop your yelling!

   b. Shall I have to muzzle you?

   c. Surely you remember that Mrs. White is sick?

3. a. Do this over!

   b. Is this the best you can do?

   c. Come now, we both know you can do better than that.

4. a. You told me my car was fixed!

   b. You call yourself a mechanic?

   c. Do you suppose I did something to it?

5. a. I just don't like your dress.

   b. What an ugly dress!

   c. Is that dress your favorite color?

COMPREHENSION   A. Interpretation   **5.** *Develops use of parts of speech through transformation of sequences*

DIRECTIONS: In each of the following groups of sentences, one sentence communicates the idea in a firm but polite way. Find that sentence and circle the letter in front of it.

1. a. Hey! Take your hat off!

   b. Please remove your hat.

   c. Is that hat glued on?

2. a. Close the door, please.

   b. For gosh sake, can't you close a door?

   c. You're letting the flies in.

3. a. Son, sit down.

   b. How many times do I have to tell you to sit?

   c. Come on, give your feet a rest!

4. a. You're blocking traffic.

   b. Gang way!

   c. Please step aside.

5. a. I think people who play cards waste time.

   b. Why should I play cards?

   c. I intensely dislike playing cards.

COMPREHENSION   A. Interpretation   **5.** *Develops use of parts of speech through transformation of sequences*

DIRECTIONS: In each of the following groups of sentences, one sentence communicates the idea in a very thoughtful way. Identify that sentence and circle the letter that precedes it.

1. a. Can't you hear me calling you?

   b. I need you; please come as soon as you are free.

   c. What's taking you so long?

2. a. (Silence, no words.)

   b. I'm sorry I hurt you.

   c. Why do you have to cry all the time?

3. a. This just won't do; you'll have to do it over.

   b. Do you think you could improve on this?

   c. It's all wrong!

4. a. Why don't you do what you're told?

   b. For Pete's sake, put your coat on!

   c. You look so good and warm in that coat.

5. a. You'll become a good cook yet; practice makes perfect.

   b. Dinner is spoiled again!

   c. Can't you cook?

Name: _____ Date: _____

DIRECTIONS:

1. Someone has proposed that a piece of property be purchased by the local government. It consists of lowland and wetland. The purpose of the purchase is to reduce the risk of flooding in the area. You take a position in favor of the purchase. Now you must collect data to back up your stand.

2. Find and list below at least four sources. Give enough information about each source so that it can easily be retrieved by someone who might want to challenge your stand.

3. State how each source would back up your position.

COMPREHENSION   B. Application   1. *Uses multiple sources for documentation and support for opinion*

DIRECTIONS:

1. There is talk among the students indicating a growing dissatisfaction with the school cafeteria. You take a stand, for or against. Now you must collect data and information.

2. Find and list below at least four sources. Give enough information about each source so that it can be easily checked by anyone who would want to contradict your position.

3. State how each source would support your position.

COMPREHENSION   **B. Application**   **1.** *Uses multiple sources for documentation and support for opinion*

DIRECTIONS:

1. The Health Department wants to fluoridate the water of your locality. Take a position either for or against. Now you must arm yourself with information and data to support your opinion.

2. From at least four sources, get the data and/or information you need to prove your point. List those sources below, giving enough information about them so that they can easily be checked by anyone doubting your claims.

3. Show how each source would document or support your opinion or position.

COMPREHENSION   **B. Application   1. *Uses multiple sources for documentation and support for opinion***

DIRECTIONS:

1. The government carried on a nationwide campaign to get all school children immunized against measles, mumps, diphtheria, and other contagious diseases.

2. Your job is to discover to what extent the campaign succeeded (in your area alone, if you wish).

3. Find at least four sources that you can consult for the information and list them below. Give enough details about them so that they can easily be checked by anyone doubting your word.

4. Show how each source would support your findings and any opinion you might hold on the subject.

COMPREHENSION   B. Application   2. *Uses maps, graphs, charts, tables when appropriate in response to readings*

DIRECTIONS: A survey was taken among students of grades 7, 8, and 9. The question asked was: "Do you favor open campus at lunch time?"

Responses revealed that, of 360 seventh graders who participated in the survey, 170 were for and 190 were against. Of those in favor, 80 were girls and 90 were boys. Of those against, 90 were girls and 100 were boys. A total of 420 eighth graders responded. Of these, 190 were for: 110 girls and 80 boys. The other 230 were against: 102 girls, 128 boys. Of a total of 503 ninth graders surveyed, 300 were for and 203 against. Of those in favor, 200 were boys and 100 were girls. Of those against, 78 were girls and 125 were boys.

Make a graph, chart, or table to illustrate the above.

COMPREHENSION   B. Application   2. *Uses maps, graphs, charts, tables when appropriate in response to readings*

DIRECTIONS: The enrollment figures for School A for the current school year are: kindergarten = 205; grade 1 = 250; grade 2 = 275; grade 3 = 280; grade 4 = 302; grade 5 = 310; grade 6 = 340; grade 7 = 310; grade 8 = 330.

School B reports figures as follows: kindergarten = 190; grade 1 = 225; grade 2 = 225; grade 3 = 290; grade 4 = 270; grade 5 = 275; grade 6 = 300; grade 7 = 300; grade 8 = 290.

Make a graph, chart, or table to compare and illustrate the above.

COMPREHENSION   B. Application   2. *Uses maps, graphs, charts, tables when appropriate in response to readings*

DIRECTIONS: Your sister's wedding invitations to out-of-town guests must include directions to the church and to your home afterward.

Draw a map that will make the directions given below easier to follow.

"Coming from the north or south on Interstate 59, take Exit 10 East. This leads you onto State Route 9, which runs east and west. If coming from the south, as you exit from the Interstate, turn right onto Route 9. If coming from the north, as you exit from the Interstate, you come up to a blinker on Route 9. Turn left. Once on Route 9, after two traffic signals, take a right onto Topaz Street. All Saints Church is at the corner of Topaz and Ruby Streets, the first left after the first traffic signal on Topaz.

To get to our home, follow Ruby Street, cross Opal Street, and turn right on Pearl. The third house on the left is your destination."

DIRECTIONS: The apple crop of Brown's Apple Orchards has been as follows over the past ten years:

1970 = 1200 bushels; 1971 = 900; 1972 = 1100; 1973 = 1500; 1974 = 1400; 1975 = 1600; 1976 = 1600; 1977 = 1500; 1978 = 1650; 1979 = 1800.

Illustrate the above with a graph, table, or chart.

COMPREHENSION   B. Application   3. *Takes notes during debate and other presentations in order to summarize and respond to logic used*

DIRECTIONS: These notes were taken by a judge for a speaking competition among three finalists. After evaluating them, answer the questions below.

A	*B*	*C*
Good stage presence	Fair stage presence	Excellent stage presence!
Intro too long	Intro great	Intro to the point
Too many examples	Knows topic very well	Sounds like a con job
No sense of humor	Touch of quiet humor	Tries too hard
Did not get to the point	Got straight to point	Did he make a point?
Delivery stiff	Convincing	Sounds insincere
Conclusion off the mark	Logical conclusion	Never reached obvious conclusion

Which speaker, A or B or C, is the:

1. _____ best speaker

2. _____ most logical

3. _____ winner

4. _____ most serious

5. _____ least convincing

6. _____ best stage presence

7. _____ con artist

8. _____ too many details

9. _____ dud

COMPREHENSION   B. Application   3. *Takes notes during debate and other presentations in order to summarize and respond to logic used*

DIRECTIONS: These notes were taken while listening to a speaker.

> Presents many facts
> Most support his point, some don't
> His thinking is cloudy
> Conclusions questionable
> Mediocre presentation

Check which of the following you think apply.

a. _____ Knowledgeable

b. _____ Exciting speech

c. _____ Convincing

COMPREHENSION   B. Application   3. *Takes notes during debate and other presentations in order to summarize and respond to logic used*

DIRECTIONS: These notes were taken while listening to a debate. Consider them, and then answer the questions below.

A	*B*
Presents case A-OK	Presents case—blah
Makes 4 good points	2 out of 4 pts OK
Thinking straight	Thinking shaky
Convincing	Appealing as a person
Conclusion sound, flows from premise	Botched the conclusion

1. If you had judged the debate, who would have won? _____

2. Why? Base your answer on the notes. _____

COMPREHENSION   B. Application   3. *Takes notes during debate and other presentations in order to summarize and respond to logic used*

DIRECTIONS: These notes were taken while listening to a political speaker on television. Ponder them, and then answer the questions that follow.

> For lower taxes
> For less government regulations
> Against equal rights
> Against his opponent
> He's the man for the job
> Didn't say which, how
> Hear! Hear!
> Didn't say why
> Naturally!
> He says!

Are the following True or False?

1. _____ The listener was in total agreement with the speaker.

2. _____ The speaker gave good reasons for his positions.

3. _____ The listener was critical and sarcastic.

COMPREHENSION   **B. Application**   **4. *Uses reading for different purposes***
                                                a. practical information
                                                b. problem solving
                                                c. recreation

DIRECTIONS: When you read for practical information, you read to find specific information on something you want to know or should know; when you read for problem solving, you read what you need to know to solve the problem; when you read for recreation, you read for the sheer enjoyment of it.

Can you tell when you are browsing among books what purpose reading a certain book might serve? Use the letters a (practical information), b (problem solving), and c (recreation), as above, to indicate what purpose the books listed below would fill.

1. _____ medical encyclopedia

2. _____ *Peanuts Birthday Book*

3. _____ *Life and Times of Woodrow Wilson*

4. _____ *U.S. Postal and Zip Code Directory*

5. _____ *History of Rome*

6. _____ book of etiquette

7. _____ English-Spanish dictionary

8. _____ *Centennial*

9. _____ *You and the Law*

10. _____ *Crafts and Hobbies*

Name: _____ Date: _____

COMPREHENSION   B. Application   **4. *Uses reading for different purposes***
                                       a. practical information
                                       b. problem solving
                                       c. recreation

DIRECTIONS: For each situation in column A, select the reading source in column C that will meet it. Place the letter of the item in column C next to the number in column A. In column B, indicate with the letters a, b, or c whether the purpose is (a) practical information, (b) problem solving, or (c) recreation. If you think there is more than one purpose, put the letter of the more important one first.

A	*B*	*C*
1. _____ Biography of someone in aviation	_____	A. encyclopedia
2. _____ How to repair an electric plug	_____	B. dictionary
3. _____ What day of the week your birthday will fall on next year	_____	C. fiction reading list
	_____	D. biography reading list
4. _____ Laws that govern magnetism		
	_____	E. calendar
5. _____ Area code for Buffalo, N.Y.		
	_____	F. *Popular Mechanics*
6. _____ A mystery thriller		
	_____	G. *Sports Illustrated*
7. _____ Definition of *thanatopsis*		
	_____	H. "how to" book
8. _____ The latest mechanical gadget someone has invented		
	_____	I. telephone directory
9. _____ Information about the printed circuit		
	_____	J. science textbook
10. _____ The currently most popular hero in the sports world		

COMPREHENSION   **B. Application**   4. *Uses reading for different purposes*
      a. practical information
      b. problem solving
      c. recreation

DIRECTIONS: For each situation in column A, select the reading source in column C that will meet it. Place the letter of the item in column C next to the number in column A. In column B, indicate with a, b, or c whether the purpose is (a) practical information, (b) problem solving, or (c) recreation. If you think there is more than one purpose, put the letter of the more important one first.

	A	*B*	*C*
1. _____	How to lengthen a dress and/or pants.	_____	A. *Atlas of the World*
2. _____	Your mother is on a diet. You want to surprise her with a meal.	_____	B. *The Joy of Cooking*
3. _____	You went hunting and got a deer. Now, how do you cook it?	_____	C. telephone directory
4. _____	Where is Mount Rushmore?	_____	D. almanac
5. _____	Who was Enrico Caruso?	_____	E. *Gray's Anatomy*
6. _____	You're sending the mayor an invitation to his home address which you don't know.	_____	F. *Weight Watcher's Cool Book*
7. _____	What and where is the peritoneum and what is its function?	_____	G. *Complete Guide to Sewing*
8. _____	What is a good program to watch tonight?	_____	H. encyclopedia, Vol. C
9. _____	Who were the winners of the baseball World Series?	_____	I. science fiction novel
10. _____	What is a book with which to fill an evening; something light with science in it?	_____	J. *You and the Law*
		_____	K. *TV Guide*

Name: _____ Date: _____

COMPREHENSION   B. Application   4. *Uses reading for different purposes*
                                             a. practical information
                                             b. problem solving
                                             c. recreation

DIRECTIONS: For each situation in column A, select the reading matter in column C that will meet it. In column B, indicate with a, b, or c whether the purpose is for (a) practical information, (b) problem solving, or (c) recreation. If you find more than one purpose, put the letter of the more important one first.

A	B	C
1. _____ Your doctor told your father he has diverticulosis. You both want to know what that is.	_____ A.	crossword puzzle
	_____ B.	*Complete Guide to Needlework*
2. _____ You've been invited to the opera "The Barber of Seville."		
	_____ C.	book of etiquette
3. _____ Something to pass time on a plane flight	_____ D.	*Merck Manual of Diagnosis and Therapy*
4. _____ How to crochet	_____ E.	*U.S. Postal and Zip Code Directory*
5. _____ Your favorite house plant is sick.		
	_____ F.	*Rhyming Dictionary*
6. _____ Should you send a gift for a certain occasion?		
	_____ G.	*Stories of Famous Operas*
7. _____ Zip code for Akron, Ohio, to address an envelope	_____ H.	*World Atlas*
8. _____ Something to pass a pleasant, quiet evening	_____ I.	*Success with House Plants*
9. _____ A word that rhymes with "acajou"	_____ J.	globe
10. _____ Population of Afghanistan	_____ K.	biography of a person you admire

COMPREHENSION   C. Analysis   **1.** *Differentiates between types of sentences*
  a. expository
  b. narrative
  c. descriptive
  d. persuasive

DIRECTIONS: Each of the sentences below is either expository (explanatory), narrative (in a story or time sequence), descriptive (conveying a sensory impression), or persuasive in nature. Decide what kind each sentence is and indicate the kind by writing the appropriate letter before each sentence.

a. Expository   b. Narrative   c. Descriptive   d. Persuasive

1. _____ The trees glowing with color seemed to vie with each other for glory.

2. _____ The speed with which a microwave oven works will give you more time to do the things you enjoy.

3. _____ A feeling of rejection caused her depression.

4. _____ He didn't set his alarm, got up late, ran for the bus, and was late for work.

5. _____ Anxiety and worry can affect your digestion, so don't give in to them.

6. _____ Place settings of flowery china, sparkling crystal, and shining silverware complimented the pink tablecloth.

7. _____ A small pillow in the curve of your back will make you more comfortable.

8. _____ He was unrecognizable in an overcoat three sizes too big and a hat likewise.

9. _____ Too much of anything palls after a while and is paid for one way or another.

10. _____ It was raining all during the homecoming game and we got soaked, but we had a hilarious time.

11. _____ They left together in a yellow pickup truck.

COMPREHENSION   **C. Analysis**   **1.** *Differentiates between types of*
sentences
a. expository
b. narrative
c. descriptive
d. persuasive

DIRECTIONS: Each of the sentences below is either expository (explanatory), narrative (in a story or time sequence), descriptive (conveying a sensory impression), or persuasive in nature. Decide what kind each sentence is and indicate the kind by writing the appropriate letter before each sentence.

a. Expository   b. Narrative   c. Descriptive   d. Persuasive

1. _____ One does not spare oneself if one loves.

2. _____ The long, bright days of summer are fading into the gloomy ones of autumn.

3. _____ On Saturday morning, they left at ten to go to visit their son at college.

4. _____ You will succeed if you give it all you've got.

5. _____ A faithful friend is a sturdy shelter.

6. _____ Love never does what is discourteous.

7. _____ She is found smiling in bright or cloudy weather, in sunshine or in rain.

8. _____ At night, the suspension cables of the bridge glow like diamond necklaces.

9. _____ A minute after the blast, we heard the sirens of the fire engines heading in the direction of it.

10. _____ Nothing in life is more wonderful than faith.

11. _____ It is indeed a beautiful pen and it is guaranteed for life.

12. _____ We returned at midnight after a long, tiring trip.

COMPREHENSION   C. Analysis   1. *Differentiates between types of sentences*
     a. expository
     b. narrative
     c. descriptive
     d. persuasive

DIRECTIONS: Each of the sentences below is either expository (explanatory), narrative (in a story or time sequence), descriptive (conveying a sensory impression), or persuasive in nature. Decide what kind each sentence is and indicate the kind by writing the appropriate letter before each sentence.

a. Expository   b. Narrative   c. Descriptive   d. Persuasive

1. _____ Buy one of these lighters; it never fails to work.

2. _____ There is not enough darkness in all the world to put out the light of one small candle.

3. _____ As the twig is bent, so will grow the tree.

4. _____ The budding leaves with their green veiled the winter nudity of the trees.

5. _____ If you go to bed early, you'll get more sleep and feel much better in the morning.

6. _____ She is a tall, willowy blonde.

7. _____ Why wear yourself out by running so hard?

8. _____ John ran away from the dog, tripped, fell, and broke his ankle.

9. _____ They cruised down the Mississippi River on the Delta Queen.

10. _____ Your money will earn higher interest at Bank A than at Bank B.

11. _____ Did he ever look smart in his white suit!

COMPREHENSION   C. Analysis   **1. *Differentiates between types of sentences***
                              a. expository
                              b. narrative
                              c. descriptive
                              d. persuasive

DIRECTIONS: Each of the sentences below is either expository (explanatory), narrative (in a story or time sequence), descriptive (conveying a sensory impression), or persuasive in nature. Decide what kind each sentence is and indicate the kind by writing the appropriate letter before each sentence.

         a. Expository   **b.** Narrative   **c.** Descriptive   **d.** Persuasive

1. _____ If not taken care of, even a small infection will fester and get worse.

2. _____ The road became slippery from the ash that fell from the belching volcano.

3. _____ Imitation is the sincerest form of flattery even if unintended as such.

4. _____ It rained the day we drove through the Petrified Forest.

5. _____ If you want to save time, consider investing in a computer; your work will go much faster.

6. _____ He is six feet tall, broad shouldered, and as handsome as a Greek god.

7. _____ The door banged, the glass in it broke, and pieces went flying in every direction.

8. _____ A foghorn warns sailors to practice extreme caution.

9. _____ After the ice storm, each tree limb was outlined in ice that sparkled in the sun.

10. _____ Butch, although an old dog, ran around like a young puppy when Andy came home.

Name: _____ Date: _____

COMPREHENSION   D. Synthesis   1. *Extends generalizations beyond sources*
2. *Hypothesizes*
3. *Suggests alternatives and options*

DIRECTIONS: Read the information below and then respond to the questions.

Nationalism is the feeling that moves individuals of one nation to put their own national interests above those of other nations or even above the common interests of all nations. This feeling has influenced certain small groups to blackmail the world and to hold it captive to their demands. While doing this to others, they deny them the very freedom they pretend to defend.

1. Extend the generalizations by indicating if the statements are true or false.

The blackmailers:

    a. _____ are true freedom fighters

    b. _____ envy the affluence of other nations which they do not have

    c. _____ are looking for freedom themselves

    d. _____ have so little, they have nothing to lose

They:

    e. _____ are being used by super powers

    f. _____ are spurred on by the reporting of the media

    g. _____ really believe they are right and the others wrong

    h. _____ trust no one

2. Check those you agree with. Let us hypothesize:

    a. _____ They really want peace.

    b. _____ They want to live better than they do.

    c. _____ They want a more democratic form of government.

    d. _____ They are being manipulated by other powers.

3. Check the alternatives you consider proper:

    a. _____ Invade them, subdue them.

    b. _____ Offer financial, material support.

    c. _____ Through peaceful means, help them get what they want.

    d. _____ Use the United Nations to help them.

COMPREHENSION   **D. Synthesis**   1. *Extends generalizations beyond sources*
2. *Hypothesizes*
3. *Suggests alternatives and options*

DIRECTIONS: Read the information below and then respond to the questions.

You haven't heard of hydroponics (hi drə pon′ iks) yet? It is the cultivation of plants without soil in water to which nutrients have been added. Experimentation with it, which began back in 1929, is now at an advanced stage and holds out great hope for the future. Hydroponics permits the growing of plants closer together than in a field. It also facilitates multiple cropping, the growing of several crops in the same tanks. The imagination is aroused to the possibilities.

1. Indicate with a "+" which items below extend the generalizations.

Hydroponics could:

    a. _____ increase the yield of crops

    b. _____ conserve the soil

    c. _____ eliminate problems of weeds and pests

    d. _____ be inexpensive

    e. _____ not require specially trained personnel

    f. _____ eliminate food waste

2. Check with a "+" those you consider worthy hypotheses:

    a. _____ Hydroponics would mean cleaner crops.

    b. _____ It could eradicate famine.

    c. _____ Each family with its own tank could grow its own food.

    d. _____ It would make present farms unnecessary.

3. Check the alternatives there might be to hydroponics food with a "+":

    a. _____ food in capsule form

    b. _____ food grown in present manner but more of it

    c. _____ more widespread famine

    d. _____ cessation of experimentation

    e. _____ more freeze-dried food

COMPREHENSION   D. Synthesis   1. *Extends generalizations beyond sources*
2. *Hypothesizes*
3. *Suggests alternatives and options*

DIRECTIONS: Read the information below and then respond to the questions.

Is there a robot in your future? With growing evidence of lower productivity, with statistics establishing the birth rate on a downward trend, is it conceivable that a situation could come about which will not only make robots necessary but also highly welcome? If we are going to continue wanting to live with the conveniences we appear most reluctant to do without, and if there are to be fewer people around to produce the conveniences and to service them, where shall we turn?

1. Indicate with a "+" which items below extend the generalizations:

    a. _____ We could all do things for ourselves.

    b. _____ We could turn back the clock to simpler times.

    c. _____ We could do without many so-called conveniences.

    d. _____ We can continue to progress.

2. Check with a "+" the following items you consider to be good hypotheses:

    a. _____ We make use of robots.

    b. _____ We can program them very precisely to do certain tasks.

    c. _____ We assign them tedious, repetitive, mechanical tasks.

    d. _____ We keep human beings free for the jobs that require judgment.

3. Check with a "+" the alternatives to the use of robots:

    a. _____ We content ourselves with lower productivity.

    b. _____ We search for other means.

    c. _____ We increase the birth rate.

    d. _____ We outlaw retirement.

Name: _____ Date: _____

COMPREHENSION   **D. Synthesis**   1. *Extends generalizations beyond sources*
    2. *Hypothesizes*
    3. *Suggests alternatives and options*

DIRECTIONS:

1. Extend the general statement that follows with a generalization or two of your own: There is no doubt that the world needs new energy-producing sources and that they are needed in a hurry.

a. _____

b. _____

c. _____

2. Now, let us suppose (hypothesize) that ...

a. _____

b. _____

c. _____

3. Alternatives or options could be ...

a. _____

b. _____

c. _____

COMPREHENSION   **E. Critical Evaluation**   1. *Develops own criteria for critical review of materials*
a. fiction   **d.** essays
b. propaganda **e.** journals
c. nonfiction   **f.** biographies

DIRECTIONS: Determine if the criteria offered are proper for evaluating the effectiveness of the kind of material indicated. Write "OK" in the space provided if a particular criterion is proper. If it is not, leave the space blank. Add at least one more criterion of your own, two if you can.

1. Propaganda about the deadly effect of drugs

   a. _____ Based on scientific evidence

   b. _____ Proof is part of the message

   c. _____ Appeals to common sense, to reason

   d. _____ Plays on fear

   e. _____ Message is complicated

   f. _____ Message is difficult to understand

   g. _____ Format is eye-catching

   h. _____ Color is used well

   i. _____ Message is insulting

   j. _____ Message appeals to all for help in the combat

   _____

   _____

2. A fiction book about teenagers and their adventures

   a. _____ Level of reading appropriate

   b. _____ Story unfolds in lifelike manner

   c. _____ Characters not really like teenagers

   d. _____ Action moves fast

   e. _____ Incidents are entertaining

   f. _____ Thread of the action hard to keep track of

   g. _____ Not illustrated

   h. _____ Author has received awards for adult fiction

   i. _____ Author has a way with words

   _____

   _____

COMPREHENSION   E. Critical Evaluation   **1. *Develops own criteria for critical review of materials***
a. fiction   **d.** essays
b. propaganda   **e.** journals
c. nonfiction   **f.** biographies

DIRECTIONS: Determine if the criteria offered are proper for evaluating the effectiveness of the kind of material indicated. Write "OK" in the space provided if a particular criterion is proper. It it is not, leave the space blank. Add at least one more criterion of your own, two if you can.

1. An essay on environmental pollution

   a. _____ Exaggerates
   b. _____ Interesting
   c. _____ Easy to read
   d. _____ Some examples given are far-fetched
   e. _____ Conclusion logical
   f. _____ Some examples true to life
   g. _____ Illustrations prove point being made
   h. _____ Strays to other pet peeves now and then
   i. _____ Contains important message

   _____

   _____

2. A nonfiction book about life in the 14th century

   a. _____ Author does historical research
   b. _____ Persons written about appear to be like people today
   c. _____ There are so many details, the reader tends to want to skip some
   d. _____ Many notes give the sources information came from
   e. _____ Author writes well
   f. _____ Maps of the time replicated
   g. _____ Book has 876 pages
   h. _____ Drawings of tools and utensils of the time
   i. _____ Excellent index

   _____

   _____

COMPREHENSION   **E. Critical Evaluation**   1. *Develops own criteria for critical review of materials*
a. fiction   **d.** essays
b. propaganda   **e.** journals
c. nonfiction   **f.** biographies

DIRECTIONS: Determine if the criteria offered are proper for evaluating the effectiveness of the kind of material indicated. Write "OK" in the space provided if a particular criterion is proper. If it is not, leave the space blank. Add at least one more criterion of your own, two if you can.

1. A journal by a country antique dealer

 a. _____ Dealer is a retired newspaperman
 b. _____ Writes with a sense of humor
 c. _____ Entertaining
 d. _____ Factual; based on true facts, he claims
 e. _____ Print is hard to read
 f. _____ Comments reveal author's outlook on life
 g. _____ Book jacket attractive
 h. _____ Interesting because the people written about are interesting
 i. _____ No illustrations
 j. _____ Reader is left wanting more

_____

_____

2. Biography of a World War II general

 a. _____ Author was his aide de camp
 b. _____ Author had access to military files and personal papers
 c. _____ Interesting
 d. _____ Fast moving
 e. _____ Point of view is not objective
 f. _____ Follows chronological order
 g. _____ Ideas flow easily from author's pen
 h. _____ Subject of biography made to appear very human
 i. _____ Lack of notes frustrating

_____

_____

COMPREHENSION   **E. Critical Evaluation**   **1.** *Develops own criteria for
critical review of materials*
a. fiction   **d.** essays
b. propaganda   **e.** journals
c. nonfiction   **f.** biographies

DIRECTIONS: Determine if the criteria offered are proper for evaluating the effectiveness of the kind of material indicated. Write "OK" in the space provided if a particular criterion is proper. If it is not, leave the space blank. Add at least one more criterion of your own, two if you can.

1. Propaganda about a new automobile

   a. _____ Clever

   b. _____ Attracts attention

   c. _____ Good print, easy to read

   d. _____ Claims are unrealistic; no proof offered

   e. _____ Car manufacturer praises car, biased

   f. _____ No mention of tests having been made, or results

   g. _____ On closer inspection, appears like a "put-on," a "set-up"

   h. _____ Appearing in a reputable publication

   i. _____ Leaves one unconvinced

_____

_____

2. Fiction book about a set of twins, male and female, who play detective

   a. _____ Book jacket attractive

   b. _____ Author is successful mystery writer

   c. _____ Events move fast

   d. _____ Dialogue and conversation are life-like

   e. _____ Suspense builds well

   f. _____ Some incidents are improbable

   g. _____ Descriptions are vivid

   h. _____ Characters are real

   i. _____ Print used is easy to read

   j. _____ Solution of mystery is a complete surprise

_____

_____

COMPREHENSION   E. Critical Evaluation   2. *Makes judgments about author's qualifications*

DIRECTIONS: Read the following items. From the information provided make a judgment about the author's qualifications for writing the work indicated. If you think the author is qualified, write "Q" in the space provided. If the author does not seem qualified, write "U."

1. _____ Bruce Bigger, who weighs over 500 pounds, has announced his intention to write a book on how to stay trim.

2. _____ Bette Bloop, a country singer, will review the operas to be performed by the touring Opera Company.

3. _____ An insurance salesman, Jim Galgan, is the author of a book entitled *Why Women Need Insurance.*

4. _____ An article on tennis appeared in "Weekly Sports." It was written by boxer Jim April.

5. _____ The presidency of the United States is the subject of a featured article in tonight's paper. Its author is former president Gerald Ford.

6. _____ "What you get out of playing football" is the subject of an article to appear soon in a sports magazine. It is to be the work of Joe Namath, former football superstar.

7. _____ Edith Foot, prominent clothing designer for female film and television stars, gives advice to home sewers in a current pattern magazine.

8. _____ George Dupe, who preferred being in the library to any other place both in high school and in college, is to author a book on library science.

9. _____ A housewife from Albuquerque, who has a degree in horticulture, is writing a book on desert flowers.

10. _____ Slim Round, a butcher, will autograph his book, "Meatless Meals," next Thursday at the mall.

COMPREHENSION   E. Critical Evaluation   2. *Makes judgments about author's qualifications*

DIRECTIONS: Read the following items. From the information provided make a judgment about the author's qualifications for writing the work indicated. If you think the author is qualified, write "Q" in the space provided. If the author does not seem qualified, write "U."

1. _____ "Philosophy of the Absurd" is the soon-to-be-published work of the humorist Steve Hopeless.

2. _____ Pete Blowhard, veteran theater reviewer, wrote the account of the last heavyweight boxing championship match.

3. _____ A local television weather man has written a review of a book entitled *How Sunspots Can Affect the Weather.*

4. _____ Championship chess player Rudolf Zink is writing a science textbook.

5. _____ *Women's Clothes, Short or Long* is a new book written by Mike Blain, a steelworker.

6. _____ The sermons of the late Reverend Brown have just been published.

7. _____ A sixteen-year-old high school student has created a comic character based on a high school teacher.

8. _____ The review of the ballet *Swan Lake* was authored by a former rock drummer.

9. _____ Jane October, a young housewife, has plans to write a book called *Problems of the Woman Executive.*

10. _____ The author of several children's books spoke at the annual Friends of the Library Luncheon on "How I Write My Books."

COMPREHENSION   **E. Critical Evaluation**   **2. *Makes judgments about author's qualifications***

DIRECTIONS: Read the following items. From the information provided make a judgment about the author's qualifications for writing the work indicated. If you think the author is qualified, write "Q" in the space provided. If the author does not seem qualified, write "U."

1. _____ Gail Sedge, tennis star, will be awarded a prize for her book *Winning Tennis at Wimbledon.*

2. _____ Ethel Quark, who lives in a land-locked state, has plans to write a book called *Every Day We Sail the Ocean.*

3. _____ The article on "Dripless Candles" in a current women's magazine is the work of a candlemaker.

4. _____ A superintendent of school's entire speech on the declining scores of students on college entrance examinations is reported in the Sunday paper.

5. _____ A school guidance counselor, Mary Bennett, has agreed to coauthor a book on *Planet Exploration.*

6. _____ Baseball umpire Dick Glove is writing a book called *Refereeing Basketball.*

7. _____ A critical review of *The Effects of Pain* was written by Josephine Lade, bedridden for the last 12 years.

8. _____ *Retirement, Plan for It* is a new book by a nineteen-year-old author.

9. _____ *How to Invest in the Stock Market*, work of the stockbroker Ray Bishop, is selling very well.

10. _____ *The Art of Makeup* is the work of ice hockey player Roger Brun.

COMPREHENSION   E. Critical Evaluation   2. *Makes judgments about author's qualifications*

DIRECTIONS: Read the following items. From the information provided make a judgment about the author's qualifications for writing the work indicated. If you think the author is qualified, write "Q" in the space provided. If the author does not seem qualified, write "U."

1. _____ A pianist of renown has published *So You Want to Play the Piano?*

2. _____ The review on "Motor Vehicle Laws Revised" was the work of the Commissioner of Motor Vehicles.

3. _____ *How to Build Your Wardrobe Inexpensively* is a new release by the millionairess Jessica Land.

4. _____ The article under the headline "Smoking Proven Harmful" was written by the Surgeon General of the United States.

5. _____ *Capture of Public Enemy No. 1* is the work of a former FBI agent.

6. _____ "Redwood Forest Glories," an article in a family magazine, had as its author the famous nature photographer Cassopic.

7. _____ Cassopic also wrote "The Philosophy of War."

8. _____ *Surviving Crises with Children*, a book by the well-known bachelor Chuck Goosenberry, is not selling well.

9. _____ A recent effort of Richard L. Bishop, M.D., Professor at George University Medical School, is "The Treatment of Tension Headaches."

10. _____ Keith Sevan, star quarterback, is putting the finishing touches on a book about school discipline.

COMPREHENSION   **E. Critical Evaluation**   **3. *Judges reasonableness between statements and conclusions***

DIRECTIONS: Decide if the following conclusions are true or false based upon the information given. Write the letter T beside each conclusion you consider to be true and an F by each one you feel is false.

1. _____ Being punctual is unimportant because no one is ever on time.

2. _____ A task well done gives great satisfaction.

3. _____ As a rule, people like to receive letters.

4. _____ Athletes are usually all muscle, lack intelligence, and cannot express themselves.

5. _____ Actors and actresses are all insincere people.

6. _____ We had an early spring so summer will be very hot.

7. _____ A globe is better than a map.

8. _____ Only in the South will you find true hospitality.

9. _____ Wealth guarantees life.

10. _____ Keeping silent, although difficult, is sometimes the best course of action.

11. _____ A high forehead is a definite sign of intelligence.

12. _____ Handsome is as handsome does.

COMPREHENSION   **E. Critical Evaluation**   3. *Judges reasonableness
between statements and
conclusions*

DIRECTIONS: Decide if the following conclusions are true or false based upon the information given. Write the letter T beside each conclusion you consider to be true and an F by each one you feel is false.

1. _____ Alcide Durand is French; he cannot learn to speak English; that means Frenchmen cannot learn to speak English.

2. _____ Soccer players have to have hard heads to hit the ball with them.

3. _____ All politicians are in politics to make money.

4. _____ Laws are sometimes difficult to obey.

5. _____ An automobile is an absolute necessity for everybody.

6. _____ Especially in summer, farmers have to work hard and long.

7. _____ It doesn't take any training to be a firefighter, so anyone can be one.

8. _____ Courtesy is an indication of thoughtfulness and consideration.

9. _____ If you truly love, you want to give.

10. _____ Mary is taller than Jane, who in turn is taller than Barbara; that means Barbara is the shortest of the three.

11. _____ A diploma is just a piece of paper.

12. _____ It's what you have learned and done to earn the diploma that really counts and is truly meaningful.

COMPREHENSION   **E. Critical Evaluation**   3. *Judges reasonableness between statements and conclusions*

DIRECTIONS: Decide if the following conclusions are true or false based upon the information given. Write the letter T beside each conclusion you consider to be true and an F by each one you feel is false.

1. _____ All the kids who attend Beaver Hollow School are snobs. I know one boy who goes there and he's the biggest snob you ever met.

2. _____ There's nothing to being a parent; all they ever do is say "no" to you.

3. _____ Persons of great achievement have usually worked very hard.

4. _____ Dreams are a sure indicator of what will happen to you in the future.

5. _____ It doesn't pay to be honest; everybody I know who is honest just isn't rich.

6. _____ Exercise, if done regularly, will help keep you fit.

7. _____ Superstars in baseball, football, and basketball come by it easily, naturally, with no hard work.

8. _____ Failure never happens to hard workers.

9. _____ Money always makes people happy and content.

10. _____ For a country, vigilance is the price of freedom.

11. _____ Taking advantage of people is okay, especially if you're stronger.

12. _____ The opposite of "keep to the right" is "keep to the wrong."

COMPREHENSION   E. Critical Evaluation   3. *Judges reasonableness*
between statements and
conclusions

DIRECTIONS: Decide if the following conclusions are true or false based upon the information given. Write the letter T beside each conclusion you consider to be true and an F by each one you feel is false.

1. _____ "The only vote that is really lost is the one that was never cast."

2. _____ Not every killing is a murder.

3. _____ Baseball players all have beautiful wives.

4. _____ Jack Sinn is a firefighter; he wears red suspenders; therefore all firefighters wear red suspenders.

5. _____ All poor people are stupid.

6. _____ Some politicians are dishonest.

7. _____ Teachers teach because they can't do anything else.

8. _____ All doctors are wealthy.

9. _____ Fall came early, so winter will be very cold.

10. _____ If you are exposed to cold germs, you may catch cold.

11. _____ Fifteen minutes of reading a day over a lifetime will make the reader a knowledgeable person.

12. _____ People who live in the North are not warm and hospitable.

STUDY SKILLS   **A. Uses Thesaurus, Almanac, Atlas, Maps, and Globes**

DIRECTIONS: Indicate the reference tool you would use to find the information below. Write the appropriate letter in the space provided.

a. Almanac   b. Atlas   c. Globe   d. Map   e. Thesaurus

1. _____ Presidential election results for 1976

2. _____ Whether a road is a farm, county, state, or federal road

3. _____ The most direct road for automobile travel between New Orleans and Atlanta

4. _____ A very precise meaning of the word *payload* in the field of aviation

5. _____ The shortest route for a plane to fly from Rome to Montreal

6. _____ The members of the U.S. Cabinet

7. _____ Synonyms for the word *insanity*

8. _____ The flag of the Upper Volta

9. _____ How many rivers are called Snake River and their locations

10. _____ The major rivers of Asia

Name: _____ Date: _____

STUDY SKILLS   A. Uses Thesaurus, Almanac, Atlas, Maps, and Globes

DIRECTIONS: Indicate the reference tool you would use to find the information below. Write the appropriate letter in the space provided.

a. Almanac   b. Atlas   c. Globe   d. Map   e. Thesaurus

1. _____ The country in which Kamaiki Point is located

2. _____ The land and sea areas that lie between Antarctica and the Arctic Ocean

3. _____ Tracing the source and tributaries of the Mississippi River to where it empties

4. _____ Most recent facts and figures on U.S. public education

5. _____ Manmade lakes and hydroelectric plants worldwide

6. _____ The countries for which travel time would be decreased by flights over the North Pole

7. _____ Several synonyms for *neutrality*

8. _____ Planning a backpacking trip in the Appalachian Mountains

9. _____ Satellites of the solar system

10. _____ The major cities of the world

Name: _____ Date: _____

DIRECTIONS: Indicate the reference tool you would use to find the information below. Write the appropriate letter in the space provided.

a. Almanac   b. Atlas   c. Globe   d. Map   e. Thesaurus

1. _____   Synonymous expressions for *hold down a job*

2. _____   The countries that have stations in Antarctica

3. _____   Which states of the U.S. border on provinces of Canada

4. _____   Where Sri Lanka is in relation to Russia geographically

5. _____   Which western states are in the Rocky Mountains

6. _____   The area in square miles of Australia

7. _____   Verb synonyms of *stamp*

8. _____   Which rivers come together in Pittsburgh, Pennsylvania

9. _____   Nobel Prize winners

10. _____   Where Argentina and Brazil are in relation to each other geographically

Name: _____ Date: _____

STUDY SKILLS   A. Uses Thesaurus, Almanac, Atlas, Maps, and Globes

DIRECTIONS: Indicate the reference tool you would use to find the information below. Write the appropriate letter in the space provided.

a. Almanac   b. Atlas   c. Globe   d. Map   e. Thesaurus

1. _____   To get an idea of how the Mercator projection of the world looks at the poles

2. _____   A synonym for *osculate*

3. _____   The time of sunrise and sunset for tomorrow

4. _____   International time zones of the world

5. _____   Maps of all of the Caribbean Islands

6. _____   Where China is in relation to the U.S. geographically

7. _____   Calendar of religious holidays

8. _____   Tracing the route of Lewis and Clark's expedition

9. _____   Index of United States colleges and universities

10. _____   The U.S. city closest to a Mexican city

Name: _____ Date: _____

STUDY SKILLS   B. Uses Variety of Media to Complete Assignments
                     and Purposes

DIRECTIONS: You have been given a topic to research and write about. Assuming that all of the resources listed immediately below are available to you, which should you consult for a complete and thorough job? Indicate those you would use and how you would use them.

almanac   card catalog   diorama   journals   newspapers
art work   cassettes   encyclopedia   magazines   photographs
atlas   computer   films   maps   resource persons
audio tapes   diaries   filmstrips   microfiche   trips
books   dictionary   globe   microfilm   TV programs

Select two out of the following three topics.

Topic 1: Volcano eruptions within the last 25 years

Topic 2: The 1996 Olympics—Winter and Summer

Topic 3: A career that attracts me

STUDY SKILLS   **B. Uses Variety of Media to Complete Assignments
and Purposes**

DIRECTIONS: You have been given a topic to research and write about. Assuming that all of the resources listed immediately below are available to you, which should you consult for a complete and thorough job? Indicate those you would use and how you would use them.

almanac	card catalog	diorama	journals	newspapers
art work	cassettes	encyclopedia	magazines	photographs
atlas	computer	films	maps	resource persons
audio tapes	diaries	filmstrips	microfiche	trips
books	dictionary	globe	microfilm	TV programs

Select two out of the following three topics.

Topic 1: The United States Census (some aspect of it or a particular one)

Topic 2: The person in history I most admire

Topic 3: The laser beam

STUDY SKILLS   **B. Uses Variety of Media to Complete Assignments and Purposes**

DIRECTIONS: You have been given a topic to research and write about. Assuming that all of the resources listed immediately below are available to you, which should you consult for a complete and thorough job? Indicate those you would use and how you would use them.

almanac	card catalog	diorama	journals	newspapers
art work	cassettes	encyclopedia	magazines	photographs
atlas	computer	films	maps	resource persons
audio tapes	diaries	filmstrips	microfiche	trips
books	dictionary	globe	microfilm	TV programs

Select two out of the following three topics.

Topic 1: The scientist and his or her contribution that I believe to be most important or most beneficial to the world

Topic 2: The history of my favorite sport or hobby

Topic 3: The woman in history whom I most admire

Name: _____ Date: _____

STUDY SKILLS **B. Uses Variety of Media to Complete Assignments
and Purposes**

DIRECTIONS: You have been given a topic to research and write about. Assuming that all of the resources listed immediately below are available to you, which should you consult for a complete and thorough job? Indicate those you would use and how you would use them.

almanac	card catalog	diorama	journals	newspapers
art work	cassettes	encyclopedia	magazines	photographs
atlas	computer	films	maps	resource persons
audio tapes	diaries	filmstrips	microfiche	trips
books	dictionary	globe	microfilm	TV programs

Select two out of the following three topics.

Topic 1: Three places I want to visit and why

Topic 2: Cable television versus commercial television

Topic 3: The four freedoms: freedom of worship, freedom from fear, freedom of speech, freedom from want

STUDY SKILLS   **C. Uses Outlining and Note-Taking Skills**

DIRECTIONS: Read the following material. Then, prepare a simple outline of the material in the space provided.

College is a means, not an end. It is the road to an objective. "Why do I need college anyway?" is too often heard. The many reasons can be boiled down to two. The first, which is twofold, concerns the growth and development of the individual. Physical growth, of course, goes on unaided for the most part. More important is intellectual growth, which must catch up and keep pace with the physical. Intellectual growth results from acquiring knowledge and from the process of learning. The second reason is emotional maturation. This results from living away from home among peers, many of whom are peers only in age and in the fact of being on the same campus. Their values, their outlooks, and their goals often contradict one's own. From that so often arise the clashes and the best lessons that spur an interwoven intellectual and emotional growth. These are the lessons learned outside the classroom.

While the first reason mentioned above is often overlooked or ignored, the second is not. Often, it is a young person's only reason for going to college. It is spelled *career* and it is equated with earning a living. Everyone wants the good life. Its cost is high. Opportunities for earning that cost could result from a college degree specifically oriented to a definite profession. It could result from the "good old liberal arts" courses which many consider an excellent base for a still hazy professional goal. Look around. While there are still some individuals who succeed without college, their number lessens as the world becomes more technological and complex. These complexities in turn make greater demands on the intellect and emotions of each individual. A good preparation is paramount because the reality of life is harsh.

I.

   A.

      1.

      2.

   B.

      1.

      2.

STUDY SKILLS   C. Uses Outlining and Note-Taking Skills

DIRECTIONS: Read the following information. Then, prepare a simple outline of the material in the space provided.

Success in college begins in the elementary grades. College freshman classes are decimated by the end of the school year. Many bright, able young people become college dropouts because they lack a realistic view of college as well as adequate preparation for it. They attend school for ten to twelve years. At some point, college beckons. After the necessary investigations, selection, and preparation for the departure, one fine fall day they find themselves on a campus.

Sinking or surviving does not depend solely on being there. Wanting to be there coupled with wanting to learn are essential. Being there can be and often is exciting and stimulating. There are so many young people to meet, all with interesting achievements to date, all with high hopes. Learning is something else. Learning demands work, often hard work, but always good work habits. Therein lies the secret to success or failure. Good work habits, specifically good study habits, cannot be purchased at the college bookstore. They are acquired like all habits, by intentional repetition of the work habits taught in the elementary grades. They are built on therefrom, growing and improving along with the individual.

An assignment given, accepted, taken seriously, and done well requires work, time, patience, and perseverance. Sometimes the most difficult part is staying glued to the chair until the task is done. There is always a plan for study that makes it a priority, includes a "where" for it, a "when," and a "how long." Students, even those with only average ability but who have excellent work habits, succeed where those lacking them, no matter how talented or how wealthy, fail.

I.

   A.

      1.

      2.

   B.

      1.

      2.

STUDY SKILLS   **C. Uses Outlining and Note-Taking Skills**

DIRECTIONS: Read the following information. Then, prepare a simple outline of the material in the space provided.

At least once a year, a newspaper headline sounds the alarm. It warns us that the world's population continues to grow but not so the world's production of food.

Miles of used-to-be farmlands have become suburban enclaves, shopping malls, and new villages. Fishermen of all nations have been forced to go farther and farther away from home shores for the "catches" that also feed. Another foe is the unreliable weather. No matter how diligently and hard the farmers work, if sun, earth, and sky do not synchronize in a manner that encourages crops to grow, human efforts are for naught. Yet, man must be fed.

While some individuals have been moaning and gnashing their teeth over the matter, technological research has been busy and is offering solutions. Technologists have found some solutions in aquaculture and hydroponics. Appropriate technology is already in use in agricultural communities in Israel and China, where food-producing carp ponds are found. A Hawaiian-based food conglomerate has teamed up with some defense electronics specialists in New Hampshire to come up with a commercially sized "lobster hotel," which will soon have an impact on the availability and cost of this highly prized and highly priced shellfish. In Arabian lands notorious for desert sands, computerized sensor-activated hydroponic systems are already productive. These systems feed plants from liquid nutrients and can, for example, produce from eight to twelve crops of tomatoes a year. Similar systems can function in cement-covered cities where land is not available.

I.
  A.

    1.

  B.

    1.

    2.

  C.

II.
  A.

    1.

    2.

  B.

    1.

181

DIRECTIONS: Read the following information. Then, prepare a simple outline of the material in the space provided.

Prophets of doom, who saw no viable commercial future for gasohol as a contributor to energy conservation, are being proven wrong. The rising cost of petroleum, an initial stimulus for the search for alternatives, has not taken any marked downward slide. It therefore remains a compelling factor. The part of the picture that is changing, however, is the wholesale price of gasohol which is becoming more competitive with that of gasoline. The U.S. Agriculture Secretary reported recently that gasohol is being produced for 98 cents per gallon wholesale. That is 3 cents above the wholesale price of unleaded gasoline, which is currently at 95 cents per gallon wholesale. The 3 cents difference is less than the 4 cents per gallon federal gasoline tax exemption given gasohol. As a result, gasoline and gasohol are running neck-and-neck.

Gasohol could easily pull ahead. Tests conducted by agencies, both public and private, have proven the ability of gasohol to improve both mileage and performance of passenger vehicles without engine modification. Additional incentives are provided by the new Energy Security Act. These should help to reach the 1982 production goal of 900 million gallons of fuel alcohol.

I.

    A.

    B.

        1.

        2.

    C.

II.

    A.

        1.

        2.

        3.

    B.

STUDY SKILLS   **C. Uses Outlining and Note-Taking Skills**

DIRECTIONS: Study the following passage and take notes so that you would be able to answer questions about it.

Etiquette is a word that isn't heard much any more. Dating back to 1607, it takes its name from the collection of rules made for the court of King Philip the Good. Included in the collection were such items as who outranked whom, as well as particular behavior expected on specified occasions. Obviously, it was for the rich and the well-born. On that basis, one should perhaps not decry its demise.

Someone has suggested that etiquette be equated with "attractive behavior." As such, it includes good manners but goes further. Basically, attractive behavior and good manners concern relationships among human beings. A fundamental truth is at its core: the moral concept of consideration for others which some call being charitable.

Whatever one chooses to call them, attractive behavior and good manners are an outward manifestation of respect for the human and personal rights of each and every individual, regardless of age, race, religion, sex, or status in life. The well-mannered, courteous person by such conduct radiates an attitude of acceptance, of concern, of caring, and of unselfishness which puts people at ease no matter what the occasion.

Such an attitude makes learning rigid rules for this or that occasion superfluous. Being mindful of others, of their rights, and of the burdens each carries, results in naturally doing what will help and avoiding what will hurt. It eliminates effrontery, insults, pushing, and shoving. These are replaced by a sharing of the burden of each and of all.

NOTES:

STUDY SKILLS   C. Uses Outlining and Note-Taking Skills

DIRECTIONS: Study the following passage and take notes so that you would be able to answer questions about it.

We all want a lot out of life. Are we, however, prepared to meet the price tag? That expression generally brings the dollar sign to mind. We realize readily enough that if we covet wheels to get around with, there's a fancy price tag on that and on every service necessary to keep the wheels going. Certainly, with a home, the price tag hits us every time the rent or the mortgage come due. What we are usually unprepared for are the price tags that go with the intangibles of life: learning, friendship, achievement, success, failure, love, hate, happiness, sorrow, prestige, family, renown, popularity, solitude. They, too, have price tags, in almost every form other than the dollar. The coin called for is likely to be time. Sometimes it is loneliness, or self, or pride, or tears, or work, or sweat, or pain, or disappointment, or frustration, or even self-denial. There is nothing for nothing. For everything we get, we give something in return. We pay a price, sometimes knowingly and willingly, other times unknowingly and unwillingly. We don't realize that the price for the sunny days is the rainy ones. Without them, the sunny days shine on a desert.

NOTES:

STUDY SKILLS   **C. Uses Outlining and Note-Taking Skills**

DIRECTIONS: Study the following passage and take notes so that you would be able to answer questions about it.

Is there really and truly such a thing as sportsmanship? It is offered as one of the important reasons for intramural and interscholastic sports. These sports, parents and taxpayers who foot the bill are told, will give their children opportunities to work off some of that extra teenage energy, contribute to physical development, and teach teamwork and sportsmanship. That is the kind of offer only an unconverted Scrooge could refuse.

The existence of sportsmanship is questioned when fights break out during or after a game. The lessons of sportsmanship have not been learned well when tempers are not kept on a leash. Sportsmanship is dealt severe blows at times by so-called professional athletes. One such example is the hero of the winning team of a recent World Series. The man was not content to have won, not sportsmanlike enough to say that his team had met and defeated a worthy opponent. That would have been true sportsmanship. Instead, at the height of the victory celebrations, the man used a vulgar expression in regard to former winners and contenders. If winning cannot make one magnanimous and able to regard losing without bitterness, what is sportsmanship? Of what value is it to have outstanding skill in a sport, to be a clever strategist in that sport, to be "big league," if at the peak of glory one stoops so low? Sportsmanship? If it exists, it is not thanks to a man like that. If it is to exist, it will have to be revived by the example of heroes worthy of the name, who know what sportsmanship is and practice it.

NOTES:

STUDY SKILLS   C. Uses Outlining and Note-Taking Skills

DIRECTIONS: Study the following passage and take notes so that you would be able to answer questions about it.

Those who have been there claim that, as hard as it is to believe, the paradise of the Pacific—Hawaii—does exist. Our fiftieth state, comprising eight major islands and numerous islets, lies about 2100 miles (3380 kilometers) southwest of mainland San Francisco. Honolulu, its capital, is on Oahu, the most populous and economically important of the islands. Hawaii Island is the largest and geologically the youngest of the group. Its principal city, Hilo, is famed for magnificent fields of orchids and for Volcanoes National Park. Kona, on the opposite side of Hawaii Island, boasts the historic City of Refuge, standing today as it did centuries ago in the days of Hawaii's warrior kings. The pineapple fields one associates with this corner of the world are mostly on Maui, along with rain forests and jungle waterfalls. Kauai is called the "Garden Island." Flowers of every description bloom in abundance and scent the air. Palms fringe the beaches, the mountains are velvety green, and the waters are crystal clear. It was nature's own set for the film *South Pacific*. The beauty nature lavished on these first four islands is not found on the other four: Kahoolawe, Lanai, Niihau, and Molokai. Molokai's claim to fame is the leper colony which is associated with the legendary Father Damien, a Belgian missionary. These islands are not the target of tourists like the others are. If abundant sunshine, acres upon acres of green plants, gaily colored flowers, coral beaches, rolling white surf, palm trees, and cloud-covered volcanic peaks are what constitute a paradise, then Hawaii is the place to find it.

NOTES:

Name: _____ Date: _____

DIRECTIONS: The reasons for reading are many. They generally influence the speed with which we read. Below are a number of different kinds of reading matter. Also listed are ways of reading that influence speed. Indicate the likely reading speed for each by putting the identifying letter of the speed in the space provided.

a. Slowly, carefully, deliberately
b. Skimming through until a particular wanted item is found
c. Quickly, taking it all in at one glance
d. Savoring, enjoying the words and how they are used
e. Moderately, not to waste time or to miss anything

1. _____ Newspaper headline

2. _____ "Peanuts" comic strip

3. _____ A poem that appeals to you

4. _____ Directions on medicine from the pharmacy

5. _____ A fast-moving, action-packed, mystery thriller

6. _____ A chapter in your social studies textbook

7. _____ The fifth day in a row of a continuing newspaper report on a disaster

8. _____ Instructions, with a diagram on how to assemble a bicycle

9. _____ A travel folder

10. _____ Classified ads

Name: _____ Date: _____

DIRECTIONS: The reasons for reading are many. They generally influence the speed with which we read. Below are a number of different kinds of reading matter. Also listed are ways of reading that influence speed. Indicate the likely reading speed for each by putting the identifying letter of the speed in the space provided.

   a. Slowly, carefully, deliberately
   b. Skimming through until a particular wanted item is found
   c. Quickly, taking it all in at one glance
   d. Savoring, enjoying the words and how they are used
   e. Moderately, not to waste time or to miss anything

1. _____ Stock market report (you own some stock)

2. _____ Account of a horrible accident in which someone you know was involved

3. _____ An article in a science magazine explaining how the laser beam works

4. _____ A word problem in mathematics

5. _____ A humorous editorial

6. _____ Report of a sports event you missed on TV

7. _____ Recipe for making cookies

8. _____ Instructions and layout guide for cutting out and making a pair of slacks

9. _____ An editorial that could influence your vote in an election

10. _____ The credits for a movie

STUDY SKILLS   D. Adjusts Reading Speed to Material and Purpose

DIRECTIONS: The reasons for reading are many. They generally influence the speed with which we read. Below are a number of different kinds of reading matter. Also listed are ways of reading that influence speed. Indicate the likely reading speed for each by putting the identifying letter of the speed in the space provided.

    a. Slowly, carefully, deliberately
    b. Skimming through until a particular wanted item is found
    c. Quickly, taking it all in at one glance
    d. Savoring, enjoying the words and how they are used
    e. Moderately, not to waste time or to miss anything

1. _____ Report of a volcanic eruption thousands of miles away

2. _____ Caption accompanying a picture that says much in itself

3. _____ The weather forecast

4. _____ Biography of a person you admire

5. _____ A humorous anecdote

6. _____ Directions on a test

7. _____ Report of a football game you attended

8. _____ Brief summary of what a TV program will be about

9. _____ Directions on an application for a job

10. _____ A pocket book of fiction that belongs to your kid brother

STUDY SKILLS   **D. Adjusts Reading Speed to Material and Purpose**

DIRECTIONS: The reasons for reading are many. They generally influence the speed with which we read. Below are a number of different kinds of reading matter. Also listed are ways of reading that influence speed. Indicate the likely reading speed for each by putting the identifying letter of the speed in the space provided.

      a. Slowly, carefully, deliberately
      b. Skimming through until a particular wanted item is found
      c. Quickly, taking it all in at one glance
      d. Savoring, enjoying the words and how they are used
      e. Moderately, not to waste time or to miss anything

1. _____ Instructions on how to fill out your income tax reporting form

2. _____ An invitation to a wedding

3. _____ An assignment: "Get an overview of ..."

4. _____ A magazine article assigned to be read which pertains to classroom material likely to come up in a test

5. _____ The small print on the warranty of the stereo you bought

6. _____ Report of the death of your favorite recording star

7. _____ Notes about the performers on a program

8. _____ The book of driving rules in your state (for your licensing test)

9. _____ A beautiful passage in an English assignment

10. _____ A book on which you will be required to give an oral report

STUDY SKILLS   **E. Demonstrates Independence in Locating, Selecting, and Using Materials to Own Purpose**

DIRECTIONS: This is an inventory intended to assess how well you can locate, select, and use materials successfully on your own. Perhaps you do this excellently; perhaps you need some improvement. Let's find out.

Answer the following truthfully by circling what you usually do. In some instances, more than one answer is possible.

1. I use the school library (now and then / when sent / frequently / regularly / never).

2. I use the local library (now and then / when told to / regularly / never).

3. I (know / do not know / am not sure) where the card catalog is located in the library I use.

4. The card catalog (helps / delays) me in my work.

5. I go to the library (to work / to meet my friends).

6. I (can go directly to / would have to ask directions for) the location of the encyclopedias.

7. I (can go directly to / would have to ask where to find) the biography collection.

8. I (can go directly to / would have to ask directions for) the fiction stacks.

9. I (can go directly to / would have to ask where to find) the dictionary.

10. I (can go directly to / would have to ask for) the atlas.

11. I (can go directly to / would have to ask for) the thesaurus.

12. To get information from a book, I prefer to (flip through the book / examine the table of contents / look in the index).

13. (Check all that apply.)
    In addition to the library, I find help:

    _____ in books and magazines at home

    _____ speaking to my teacher(s)

    _____ asking questions in class

    _____ discussing with classmates

    _____ thinking up unusual ways to get information

    _____ questioning adults out of school who might be expected to know something about what I'm trying to learn

14. Footnotes are (important / unimportant). I (pay / do not pay) attention to them.

15. Mark *a* (I know) or *b* (I do not know):

    _____ the purpose of a bibliography

    _____ how to use one

    _____ how to compile one

16. When I receive an assignment I (can't wait to get going / don't know where to begin).

17. Finding a source of information no one else did (never happens to me / happens occasionally to me).

18. Sometimes, because of something I've read or seen or heard, I get curious about it so I (do nothing about my curiosity / go looking for answers in books).

19. When working on an assignment, if I come upon something that is interesting but extraneous at the moment, I (pass over it and forget it / make a note of it and return to it later / read it then and there as a relaxation).

20. When I am in search of information for whatever reason, (it's always in the back of my mind / I forget about it unless I'm working on it). As a result, I (come / do not come) upon helpful information where I least expect it.

21. I (hesitate / do not hesitate) to ask for help if I get stuck or feel I'm spinning my wheels.

22. I feel I (know / do not know) how to take notes well.

23. When I find information, (I don't know what to do with it / it takes me too long to figure out how to use it / I can usually use it readily enough).

24. I (can / cannot) decide not to use information which I found but doesn't seem to fit my purpose.

25. I believe I need help with: _____

STUDY SKILLS   **F. Applies Problem-Solving Approach**

DIRECTIONS: The problem-solving approach is a very useful skill. It can be applied to many life situations, including the best way to handle a school assignment.

A. The steps needed in problem solving are listed below in jumbled order. In the space provided, write the order in which they should occur.

_____ Get all the facts together.

_____ Decide on one way to act.

_____ Ask: Just what is the problem?

_____ Ask: Did it work? Yes? Why? How well? No? Why not?

_____ Look for several ways to handle the situation.

_____ Take action.

B. The items below are the same as those above, but in simpler language. These are also jumbled. Match them by putting the numbers of the items under **A** in the space provided here. Then, rewrite the items here in the proper order.

_____ Select option   1. _____

_____ Gather information   2. _____

_____ Act   3. _____

_____ Identify problem   4. _____

_____ Evaluate   5. _____

_____ Devise possible   6. _____
        solutions

C. Now, take the first letter of the first word in the column on the right in **B** and make a sentence with words beginning with those letters. That will be your mnemonic device to remember the steps in problem solving. Write your sentence here.

_____

D. Now, memorize it!

Name: _____ Date: _____

DIRECTIONS: You get up in the morning and go into the kitchen to get your breakfast. The floor is covered with water. You keep your head. You say, "Aha! Problem solving!" Indicate the steps you take.

1. Identify problem:

2. Gather information:

3. Devise possible solutions:

4. Select option:

5. Act:

6. Evaluate:

STUDY SKILLS   **F. Applies Problem-Solving Approach**

DIRECTIONS: You go to use your car. You notice that the right front tire doesn't look right. You are planning to leave the next morning on a long trip. Apply your problem-solving skills and list what you would do.

1. Identify problem:

2. Gather information:

3. Devise possible solutions:

4. Select option:

5. Act:

6. Evaluate:

Name: _____ Date: _____

STUDY SKILLS   **F. Applies Problem-Solving Approach**

DIRECTIONS: Just as you are about to leave for school, you discover that your bicycle has apparently been stolen. You have to get to school. It's the day for final exams. Keep your cool. Use your problem-solving skills and list what you would do.

1. Identify problem:

2. Gather information:

3. Devise possible solutions:

4. Select option:

5. Act:

6. Evaluate:

Name: _____ Date: _____

DIRECTIONS: The following statements pertain to learning, which is the objective of study. Read them carefully. Indicate whether you agree or disagree by writing "A" if you agree and "D" if you disagree.

1. _____ To study is to memorize.

2. _____ There are several ways to study.

3. _____ Repetition is the mother of learning.

4. _____ To study is to apply oneself, to work at the acquisition of knowledge.

5. _____ It is useless to attempt to learn what is not first clearly understood.

6. _____ Study is earnest and careful examination of a particular question.

7. _____ Nothing enters the mind—the intellect—without first passing through the senses, that is, sight, hearing, smell, taste, touch.

8. _____ The greater the number of senses used in learning, the more effective the learning will be.

9. _____ Memorizing is only a tool for studying.

10. _____ Learning by doing is effective because it involves the whole being.

11. _____ If you can't explain it, you don't know it.

12. _____ "If at first you don't succeed, try, try again" is an important axiom to remember in studying.

STUDY SKILLS   **G. Designs, Uses, and Revises Own Study Schedules**

DIRECTIONS: There are several ways to study. Much depends on the purpose for studying, the difficulty of the subject matter, and the available time. For the situation described here, check the statements that would apply. Number them in the order in which they would be most effective.

It is Thursday the 16th. Your science teacher has announced a test on the Magnetism chapter for the following Thursday, the 23rd. Which of the following are included in your study plan?

Check   Rank

a. _____   Cancel all plans for the night of Wednesday   _____
             the 22nd.

b. _____   Study your notes and text during each study period.   _____

c. _____   Check the length of the chapter.   _____

d. _____   Estimate the total amount of time you will need   _____
             to review thoroughly.

e. _____   Check the amount of notes you have.   _____

f. _____   Plan whether or not to study on the weekend.   _____

g. _____   Plan to review notes and text only the   _____
             night before the exam.

h. _____   Plan to study a minimum of 1½ hours each day   _____
             after the evening meal.

i. _____   Keep strictly to the plan of study.   _____

j. _____   On Wednesday the 22nd, begin review.   _____

k. _____   Go to bed early on Wednesday the 22nd.   _____

l. _____   Stay up late to study on Wednesday the 22nd.   _____

STUDY SKILLS   G. Designs, Uses, and Revises Own Study Schedules

DIRECTIONS: How one studies depends on the purpose for studying and on the difficulty of the material. One plans study time accordingly. For the situation described, check the steps that would be best. Then number them to show the priority you would assign each one you checked.

You are in a branch of the military, in a special training school you requested. The instructor announces that every Friday there will be a test on the subject matter covered from Monday through Thursday. One failed test will put you on warning; the second failed test will put you out of the program. Your chances then of getting into another training program become very difficult.

Check   Rank

a. _____   Listen carefully in class.   _____

b. _____   Do not take notes; trust your memory.   _____

c. _____   One night you study; one night you don't.   _____

d. _____   Almost daily, examine carefully the duplicated notes   _____
                       handed out by the instructor.

e. _____   Plan to study long and late on Thursday night.   _____

f. _____   Discard the instructor's handouts.   _____

g. _____   Take careful notes.   _____

h. _____   Study each day's notes and instructions each night.   _____

i. _____   Keep your study schedule irregular.   _____

j. _____   Study notes and instructions every other   _____
                       night.

k. _____   Study each day's notes and review those of the   _____
                       previous day every night.

l. _____   Go to the test on Friday, relaxed and confident.   _____

m. _____   Go to the test on Friday, uptight and worried.   _____

STUDY SKILLS   **G. Designs, Uses, and Revises Own Study Schedules**

DIRECTIONS: The teacher announces on Thursday the 2nd that the final exam in math will be exactly four weeks from that day, on the 30th. The test will cover the material taught during the second half of the school year. A look at the book tells you that's a total of ten chapters. You have four weeks or 28 days, 27 not counting the test date, to prepare. What you will know will be not only what you will answer correctly on the test. It will be what you have gotten into, deeply, seriously, thoroughly.

s	m	t	w	t	f	s
			1	2	3	4
5	6	7	8	9	10	11
12	13	14	15	16	17	18
19	20	21	22	23	24	25
26	27	28	29	30	31	

Examine the options offered carefully and decide which you think is the one mostly likely to give the best results.

_____ A. Decide to review topics or chapters each day for five days before the exam.

_____ B. Decide to study only the day before the exam, staying up all night if necessary.

_____ C. Decide to review one topic a day each day during the two weeks before the exam.

_____ D. Review one chapter or topic a day for ten days;
then two a day for five days;
then three and a third a day for three days;
then five a day for two days;
then the whole in one day.
A total of 21 days will be needed.
By following this plan, you will have reviewed your material five times.

STUDY SKILLS   **H. Locates Sources Within a Book by Using Table of Contents and Index**

DIRECTIONS: Study the mini Table of Contents and Index below. Then, answer the questions that follow.

Table of Contents

Index

_____ 1. In what chapter will you find out about the clothing the Romans wore?

_____ 2. On what page will you discover the association between *calculate* and *calculus*?

_____ 3. In which chapter would you look to find the meaning of *D.C.*?

_____ 4. On which page would you look to find the meaning of *D.C.*?

_____ 5. In which section will you find items that pertain to one topic and find them together?

_____ 6. Which is given in alphabetical order, the Table of Contents or the Index?

_____ 7. In which can you quickly locate a specific item?

_____ 8. The meaning of *ex officio* will be on which page?

_____ 9. On which page will you find information about a language based on Latin, other than English?

_____ 10. What is that language?

STUDY SKILLS   **H. Locates Sources Within a Book by Using Table of Contents and Index**

DIRECTIONS: Study the mini Table of Contents and Index below. Then, answer the questions that follow.

Table of Contents

Index

_____ 1. Which, the Table of Contents or the Index, is set up in topical order rather than alphabetical order?

_____ 2. What similar item pertaining to adjectives and adverbs do you find listed under another heading?

_____ 3. In which chapter would you find information about French family life?

_____ 4. In which chapter will French influence in America be evident?

_____ 5. Under which section and on what page would you look for the names of the days of the week?

_____ 6. In which, Table of Contents or Index, will you have quicker access to grammar information?

_____ 7. What interesting item that you don't expect do you find when you look up *time*?

_____ 8. Phonetic symbols may be looked up under which two other alternatives?

_____ 9. Is there any likelihood of finding French equivalents of English names in this book?

_____ 10. For a comparison of French and American schools, will looking under "Comparison" in the Index give results?

Name: _____ Date: _____

DIRECTIONS: Study the mini Table of Contents and Index below. Then, answer the questions that follow.

_____ 1. Would you say that the use of the Table of Contents and of the Index serve the same purpose?

_____ 2. Which provides a general idea of what the book is about?

_____ 3. Which is a time-saver for spotting information quickly?

_____ 4. What makes the Index faster to use?

_____ 5. If the listings in the Index are alphabetical, what are those of the Table of Contents?

_____ 6. How many items in the Index have any connection with Chapter I?

_____ 7. Give all pages on which information on labels can be found.

_____ 8. Which chapter deals primarily with the way you dress?

_____ 9. Where will you find information on health habits? Give chapter and page.

_____ 10. Do you think that the Table of Contents and the Index complement each other?

STUDY SKILLS **H. Locates Sources Within a Book by Using Table of Contents and Index**

DIRECTIONS: Study the mini Table of Contents and Index below. Then, answer the questions that follow.

_____ 1. On which page would you find how house plants give pleasure?

_____ 2. Which chapter deals with taking care of house plants?

_____ 3. Where can one learn about a soil-testing kit?

_____ 4. You want to propagate an African violet. In which chapter and on what page will you look?

_____ 5. What other source is available to give information about upright plants?

_____ 6. True or False? A glance at the Table of Contents gives no idea of what is really in the book.

_____ 7. True or False? The Index is like a pointer which helps to find information more readily.

_____ 8. Practically all of the general information about light and its relationship to plants should be found under which section and on what page?

_____ 9. Your problem is a parched plant. What page can offer help?

_____ 10. Where would you find information about how and where to use a five-foot cactus plant?

CREATIVE READING   **A. Recognizes Figurative Language, Dialect, and Colloquial Speech**

DIRECTIONS: Classify the following statements as (a) *figurative language* (containing figures of speech such as similes or metaphors to add vividness to a description), (b) *dialect* (language peculiar to a region or group of persons), or (c) *colloquial speech* (conversational, informal language, slang). Place the appropriate letter in the space provided before each statement.

a. figurative language   b. dialect   c. colloquial speech

_____ 1. He's just a good ole' boy.

_____ 2. In its anger, the crowd roared like a lion.

_____ 3. You want I should do it for you?

_____ 4. Jack Frost used diamonds to paint the windows last night.

_____ 5. Eh Jo, my fren, you like it here, non?

_____ 6. She paarked the caar in the yaard.

_____ 7. You sure took off in a hurry.

_____ 8. Where's your pad, man?

_____ 9. We heard the motor roar furiously, then hiccup, then fall silent.

_____ 10. Y'all come back to see us now, y'hear?

_____ 11. She cradled the baby in her arms and he purred like a kitten until he fell asleep.

_____ 12. O.K., good buddy.

CREATIVE READING   **A. Recognizes Figurative Language, Dialect, and Colloquial Speech**

DIRECTIONS: Classify the following statements as (a) *figurative language* (containing figures of speech such as similes or metaphors to add vividness to a description), (b) *dialect* (language peculiar to a region or group of persons), or (c) *colloquial speech* (conversational, informal language, slang). Place the appropriate letter in the space provided before each statement.

a. figurative language   b. dialect   c. colloquial speech

_____ 1. How come you're not hungry?

_____ 2. I need some bread, man.

_____ 3. He ain't nothing but a turkey.

_____ 4. Smokey bear ahead!

_____ 5. Through the open cabin window, we could hear the lake gently lapping the shore.

_____ 6. That ol' preachin', t'warn't nothin'.

_____ 7. Woodpecker? With his rat-a-tat, rat-a-tat-tat, he's a light-machine gunner.

_____ 8. You want I should draw you a picture?

_____ 9. For Pete's sake, cut it out!

_____ 10. There was a great spotlight of Mother Nature's coming slowly up over the horizon, making a pathway of glittering sequins across the river.

_____ 11. That's a big 10-20.

_____ 12. They've gone up the road a piece.

Name: _____ Date: _____

CREATIVE READING   **A. Recognizes Figurative Language, Dialect, and Colloquial Speech**

DIRECTIONS: Classify the following statements as (a) *figurative language* (containing figures of speech such as similes or metaphors to add vividness to a description), (b) *dialect* (language peculiar to a region or group of persons), or (c) *colloquial speech* (conversational, informal language, slang). Place the appropriate letter in the space provided before each statement.

a. figurative language   b. dialect   c. colloquial speech

_____ 1. As the sun sank, it painted the western sky with yellow, then orange, red, and finally deep purple.

_____ 2. Educated mebbe he is; bright, he ain't.

_____ 3. I'm sober as a judge on election day.

_____ 4. When students' eyes glow with the excitement of understanding, then the teacher knows that learning is taking root.

_____ 5. She never did take up no truck with book larnin'.

_____ 6. Isn't she a mess? I just love her!

_____ 7. A clear conscience is a treasure that cannot be weighed by a scale.

_____ 8. Aw, go fly a kite!

_____ 9. He's full of prunes.

_____ 10. Us would raise a ruckus.

_____ 11. The thunder roared and echoed as if trapped by the palisades.

_____ 12. My papa, he say, non, non, non!

CREATIVE READING   **A. Recognizes Figurative Language, Dialect, and**
                              Colloquial Speech

DIRECTIONS: Classify the following statements as (a) *figurative language* (containing figures of speech such as similes or metaphors to add vividness to a description), (b) *dialect* (language peculiar to a region or group of persons), or (c) *colloquial speech* (conversational, informal language, slang). Place the appropriate letter in the space provided before each statement.

a. figurative language   b. dialect   c. colloquial speech

_____ 1. I just ain't gonna do it!

_____ 2. Her eyes are the most gorgeous aquamarines!

_____ 3. Ah, ma Tony, he's buy me ice box. He's good boy.

_____ 4. You could follow the journey of the canal barge by just listening to it chug chugging its way into the distance.

_____ 5. In the strong wind, the trees shook off their leaves to carpet the ground.

_____ 6. Put it here, man.

_____ 7. My fren, Batiste, he not lak strangers.

_____ 8. Vot kin I tell you?

_____ 9. Hey Nell, ole girl, what's cooking?

_____ 10. That sun-filled happy morning, the chirping of the birds was music to my ears.

_____ 11. They done treat me real fine.

_____ 12. We went down the pike hell-bent for election!

CREATIVE READING   B. Understands Literary Forms   1. *Folk literature*

DIRECTIONS: Classify each of the following as (a) *tale* (story of true, legendary, or fictitious events), (b) *song* (verse set to music), (c) *fable* (fictitious story that teaches a moral lesson; characters usually are talking animals), (d) *legend* (story handed down for generations of a specific people and believed to have a historical basis), (e) *myth* (traditional story believed to have a historical basis and serving to explain some phenomenon of nature or the customs and religious rites of a people; characters usually are gods and heroes). Place the appropriate letter in the space provided before each item. You may be familiar with some. For those that are unfamiliar to you, use your skills for locating information to become acquainted. Read them to enrich your literary background.

              a. tale   b. song   c. fable   d. legend   e. myth

_____ 1. Careless Love

_____ 2. Hansel and Gretel

_____ 3. The Boy and the Wolf

_____ 4. Pygmalion

_____ 5. Murders in the Rue Morgue

_____ 6. The Country Maid and the Milk Pail

_____ 7. Bury Me Not on the Lone Prairie

_____ 8. Silver Jack

_____ 9. Jesse James

_____ 10. The Golden Fleece

_____ 11. The Wolf in Sheep's Clothing

_____ 12. Colonel Crockett and the Bear and the Swallows

CREATIVE READING   B. Understands Literary Forms   1. *Folk literature*

DIRECTIONS: Classify each of the following as (a) *tale* (story of true, legendary, or fictitious events), (b) *song* (verse set to music), (c) *fable* (fictitious story that teaches a moral lesson; characters usually are talking animals), (d) *legend* (story handed down for generations of a specific people and believed to have a historical basis), (e) *myth* (traditional story believed to have a historical basis and serving to explain some phenomenon of nature or the customs and religious rites of a people; characters usually are gods and heroes). Place the appropriate letter in the space provided before each item. You may be familiar with some. For those that are unfamiliar to you, use your skills for locating information to become acquainted. Read them to enrich your literary background.

a. tale   b. song   c. fable   d. legend   e. myth

_____ 1. Cyclops

_____ 2. The Pit and the Pendulum

_____ 3. Hercules

_____ 4. The Tricky Fox and the Stork

_____ 5. The Streets of Laredo

_____ 6. The Holy Grail

_____ 7. Down in the Valley

_____ 8. The Hare and the Tortoise

_____ 9. Rapunzel

_____ 10. Santa Claus

_____ 11. Bre'r Rabbit, Bre'r Fox and the Tar Baby

_____ 12. The Masque of the Red Death

CREATIVE READING   **B. Understands Literary Forms**   1. *Folk literature*

DIRECTIONS: Classify each of the following as (a) *tale* (story of true, legendary, or fictitious events), (b) *song* (verse set to music), (c) *fable* (fictitious story that teaches a moral lesson; characters usually are talking animals), (d) *legend* (story handed down for generations of a specific people and believed to have a historical basis), (e) *myth* (traditional story believed to have a historical basis and serving to explain some phenomenon of nature or the customs and religious rites of a people; characters usually are gods and heroes). Place the appropriate letter in the space provided before each item. You may be familiar with some. For those that are unfamiliar to you, use your skills for locating information to become acquainted. Read them to enrich your literary background.

a. tale   b. song   c. fable   d. legend   e. myth

_____ 1. Rip Van Winkle

_____ 2. Frankie and Johnny

_____ 3. The Lion and the Gnat

_____ 4. The Dog and the Shadow

_____ 5. The Cask of Amontillado

_____ 6. The Duck with the Golden Eggs

_____ 7. Pandora

_____ 8. Cinderella

_____ 9. Shenandoah

_____ 10. Evangeline

_____ 11. Sam Bass

_____ 12. The Grasshopper and the Ant

CREATIVE READING   B. Understands Literary Forms   1. *Folk literature*

DIRECTIONS: Classify each of the following as (a) *tale* (story of true, legendary, or fictitious events), (b) *song* (verse set to music), (c) *fable* (fictitious story that teaches a moral lesson; characters usually are talking animals), (d) *legend* (story handed down for generations of a specific people and believed to have a historical basis), (e) *myth* (traditional story believed to have a historical basis and serving to explain some phenomenon of nature or the customs and religious rites of a people; characters usually are gods and heroes). Place the appropriate letter in the space provided before each item. You may be familiar with some. For those that are unfamiliar to you, use your skills for locating information to become acquainted. Read them to enrich your literary background.

a. tale   b. song   c. fable   d. legend   e. myth

_____ 1. The Unicorn

_____ 2. The Golden Pot

_____ 3. Jupiter

_____ 4. The Thousand Nights and a Night

_____ 5. The Fox and the Grapes

_____ 6. Mademoiselle from Armentieres

_____ 7. Custer's Last Charge

_____ 8. The Gold Bug

_____ 9. The Adventures of Ulysses

_____ 10. Snow White

_____ 11. King Midas

_____ 12. Old Smoky

CREATIVE READING   **B. Understands Literary Forms**
                      2. *Short story*
                      3. *Nonfiction, including propaganda*
                      4. *Poetry, limerick, couplet, sonnet, blank verse,
                         and internal rhyme*

DIRECTIONS: Below are the titles of literary works. Classify each by placing the appropriate letter in the space provided. For those with which you are unfamiliar, use your skills for locating information and then classify them.

a. Short story	d. Propaganda	g. Couplet
b. Fiction	e. Poetry	h. Sonnet
c. Nonfiction	f. Limerick	i. Blank verse

_____ 1. THE GREAT STONE FACE—Nathaniel Hawthorne

_____ 2. WORKING IT OUT—Sara Ruddick and Pamela Daniels

_____ 3. ABSENCE—William Shakespeare

_____ 4. THERE WAS A YOUNG LADY FROM CORK—Ogden Nash

_____ 5. FOG—Carl Sandburg

_____ 6. DONNYBROOK—James Stephens

_____ 7. THE MORTAL INSTRUMENTS—T. Ernesto Bethancourt

_____ 8. ROLLER SKATING GUIDE—Hal Straus and Marilou Sturges

_____ 9. TREES—Joyce Kilmer

_____ 10. I'M A FOOL—Sherwood Anderson

_____ 11. LOVE—Elizabeth Barrett Browning

_____ 12. A BRANCH LIBRARY—James Montgomery Flagg

_____ 13. THE SONG OF HIAWATHA—Henry Wadsworth Longfellow

_____ 14. TIN WEDDING WHISTLE—Ogden Nash

_____ 15. MISPLACED PERSONS—Lee Harding

_____ 16. ALL THINGS BRIGHT AND BEAUTIFUL—James Herriot

_____ 17. THE SHEPHERDESS—Alice Meynell

_____ 18. COMMON SENSE—Thomas Paine

_____ 19. THE MAN WITHOUT A COUNTRY—Edward Everett Hale

_____ 20. TO HIS LOVE—William Shakespeare

Name: _____ Date: _____

CREATIVE READING   **B. Understands Literary Forms**
                          2. *Short story*
                          3. *Nonfiction, including propaganda*
                          4. *Poetry, limerick, couplet, sonnet, blank verse, and internal rhyme*

DIRECTIONS: Below are the titles of literary works. Classify each by placing the appropriate letter in the space provided. For those with which you are unfamiliar, use your skills for locating information and then classify them.

a. Short story	d. Propaganda	g. Couplet
b. Fiction	e. Poetry	h. Sonnet
c. Nonfiction	f. Limerick	i. Blank verse

_____ 1. STOPPING BY A WOODS ON A SNOWY EVENING—Robert Frost

_____ 2. MIRACLE AT CARVILLE—Betty Martin

_____ 3. THE ETRUSCAN SMILE—Velda Johnston

_____ 4. NEWS ITEM—Dorothy Parker

_____ 5. EVANGELINE—Henry Wadsworth Longfellow

_____ 6. THE CANTANKEROUS 'GATOR—Oliver Herford

_____ 7. ON HIS BLINDNESS—John Milton

_____ 8. RIDING THE NIGHTMARE—Selma R. Williams

_____ 9. TEARS—Elizabeth Barrett Browning

_____ 10. A TEACHER—Charles Battel Loomis

_____ 11. JONATHAN SWIFT SOMERS—Edgar Lee Masters

_____ 12. PASS, FRIEND—Carl Sandburg

_____ 13. HENRY STARR—LAST OF THE REAL BADMEN—Glenn Shirley

_____ 14. I HAVE A RENDEZVOUS WITH DEATH—Alan Seeger

_____ 15. LOST ISLAND—Phyllis A. Whitney

_____ 16. LEGEND OF SLEEPY HOLLOW—Washington Irving

_____ 17. DREAMING FOOL—Carl Sandburg

_____ 18. THE CHRYSANTHEMUMS—John Steinbeck

_____ 19. THE EEL—Ogden Nash

_____ 20. LETTERS TO TRACY—Don Gold

_____ 21. WHAT IS TO BE DONE—V. I. Lenin

CREATIVE READING   **B. Understands Literary Forms**
                      2. *Short story*
                      3. *Nonfiction, including propaganda*
                      4. *Poetry, limerick, couplet, sonnet, blank verse,*
                          and internal rhyme

DIRECTIONS: Below are the titles of literary works. Classify each by placing the appropriate letter in the space provided. For those with which you are unfamiliar, use your skills for locating information and then classify them.

a. Short story	d. Propaganda	g. Couplet
b. Fiction	e. Poetry	h. Sonnet
c. Nonfiction	f. Limerick	i. Blank verse

_____ 1. STILL WATERS, WHITE WATERS—Ron Fisher

_____ 2. TAVERN—Edna St. Vincent Millay

_____ 3. ON A BOXER—X. J. Kennedy

_____ 4. THE DEATH OF THE HIRED MAN—Robert Frost

_____ 5. RELATIVITY AND LEVITATION—Gelett Burgess

_____ 6. THE HUMAN SEASONS—John Keats

_____ 7. DEATHMAN, DO NOT FOLLOW ME—Jay Bennett

_____ 8. THE PRISONER—Elizabeth Barrett Browning

_____ 9. A PERSONAL EXPERIENCE—Oliver Herford

_____ 10. THE COURTSHIP OF MILES STANDISH—Henry Wadsworth Longfellow

_____ 11. REFLECTION OF BABIES—Ogden Nash

_____ 12. I AM THIRD—Gale Sayers and Al Silverman

_____ 13. BARTER—Sara Teasdale

_____ 14. A TELEPHONE CALL—Dorothy Parker

_____ 15. SEA FEVER—John Masefield

_____ 16. THREE PLAYERS OF A SUMMER GAME—Tennessee Williams

_____ 17. A STRING IN THE HARP—Nancy Bond

_____ 18. BOY FRIENDS, GIRL FRIENDS, JUST FRIENDS—A. Richards and W. Kramer

_____ 19. A WONDERFUL BIRD—Dixon Lanier Merrett

_____ 20. EVER—Carl Sandburg

_____ 21. MEIN KAMPF—Adolf Hitler

Name: _____ **Date:** _____

CREATIVE READING **B. Understands Literary Forms**
  2. *Short story*
  3. *Nonfiction, including propaganda*
  4. *Poetry, limerick, couplet, sonnet, blank verse, and internal rhyme*

DIRECTIONS: Below are the titles of literary works. Classify each by placing the appropriate letter in the space provided. For those with which you are unfamiliar, use your skills for locating information and then classify them.

a. Short story	d. Propaganda	g. Couplet
b. Fiction	e. Poetry	h. Sonnet
c. Nonfiction	f. Limerick	i. Blank verse

_____ 1. TOO YOUNG TO DIE—Francine Klagsbrun

_____ 2. TO MR. LAWRENCE—John Milton

_____ 3. DAS KAPITAL—Karl Marx

_____ 4. JANE EMILY—Lee and Shepard Lothrop, Patricia Clapp

_____ 5. FOR TRAVELERS GOING SIDEREAL—Robert Frost

_____ 6. FORGOTTEN WARS—Carl Sandburg

_____ 7. THE JELLYFISH—Ogden Nash

_____ 8. IF—Rudyard Kipling

_____ 9. THE SOLDIER—Rupert Brooke

_____ 10. EXPLODING STAR—Fritz Molden

_____ 11. THE PARENT—Ogden Nash

_____ 12. LOST—Carl Sandburg

_____ 13. THE PROVIDENT PUFFIN—Oliver Herford

_____ 14. SPRING—Gerard Manley Hopkins

_____ 15. BILLY BUDD—Herman Melville

_____ 16. ABRAHAM LINCOLN WALKS AT MIDNIGHT—Vachel Lindsay

_____ 17. BABYLON REVISITED—F. Scott Fitzgerald

_____ 18. BY THE SEA—William Wordsworth

_____ 19. PEDIATRIC REFLECTION—Ogden Nash

_____ 20. LIEF THE LUCKY—Carl Sandburg

CREATIVE READING   **C. Compares Value Systems of Characters**

DIRECTIONS: Read the following passage. Then, place a B by each word that reflects the value system of Bob. Place a J by each word that reflects the value system of Jim. If both Bob and Jim share a value, use both letters.

"Hey there, Jim! What's happening?"

"Hi, Bob! It's great to see you. How have you been? Haven't seen you in a long time, too long!"

"Good to see you too, Jim."

"I didn't know you had a car, Bob."

"Oh, it's not mine; it's my brother's. But he doesn't know I have it. Like to take a ride, Jim?"

"Gee, no thanks, Bob. If your brother doesn't know you have his car, I wouldn't feel right. Thanks for the invitation anyway. Besides, I'm late getting home as it is."

_____ 1. friendliness   _____ 7. punctuality

_____ 2. directness   _____ 8. irresponsibility

_____ 3. truthfulness   _____ 9. dishonesty

_____ 4. courtesy   _____ 10. daring

_____ 5. honesty   _____ 11. cautiousness

_____ 6. responsibility   _____ 12. risk-taking

CREATIVE READING   C. Compares Value Systems of Characters

DIRECTIONS: Read the following passage. Then, place a P by each word that reflects the value system of Peggy. Place an L by each word that reflects the value system of Louise. If both Peggy and Louise share a value, use both letters.

"Let's have a serious talk," said Peggy.

"Serious? What do we have to be serious about?" questioned her best friend, Louise.

"Well, let's talk about our future. Before we know it, we'll be graduating. We've got to be thinking ahead. What are we going to do with our lives?"

"Have as much fun as I can with mine," interrupted Louise.

"Come on. Be serious for once. We've got to think and plan so that our lives will amount to something, like in the line from the poem, 'Departing, leave behind you, footprints on the sands of time.'"

"You worry too much, Peggy. That's a long way off. Let's have fun! Now!"

"Louise, you worry me. All you ever want to talk about or think about is having fun!"

_____ 1. friendship	_____ 7. directness, forthrightness
_____ 2. fun-loving	_____ 8. honesty
_____ 3. prudence	_____ 9. carefree
_____ 4. caring	_____ 10. worry
_____ 5. concern	_____ 11. foresight
_____ 6. seriousness	_____ 12. purposefulness

CREATIVE READING   C. Compares Value Systems of Characters

DIRECTIONS: Read the following passage. Then, place a P by each word that reflects the value system of Paul. Place an L by each word that reflects the value system of Lee. If Paul and Lee share a value, use both letters.

"Let's go to the library, Lee, to see what new science magazines have come in."

"Paul, if I go to the library with you, you read the science magazines. I'll get me a comic book," Lee replied.

"Since when have you been reading them?" asked Paul with emphasis on "them."

"Since I decided all work and no play will make Lee a dull boy."

"Lee, since when has going to the library as we've been doing for years now become work?"

"Oh, come on, Paul. I was just teasing. You know I'm just as much a nut about those science magazines as you are!"

_____ 1. companionship   _____ 7. playfulness

_____ 2. caring   _____ 8. love of science

_____ 3. seriousness   _____ 9. good habits

_____ 4. studiousness   _____ 10. fun-loving

_____ 5. earnestness   _____ 11. not wasting time

_____ 6. curiosity   _____ 12. yielding

CREATIVE READING   C. Compares Value Systems of Characters

DIRECTIONS: Read the following passage. Then, place an A by each word that reflects the value system of Alice. Place an E by each word that reflects the value system of Eva. If Alice and Eva share a value, use both letters.

"What's wrong with smoking?" Alice asked of her long-time friend, Eva.

"It can ruin your health. Maybe not today, maybe not tomorrow, but in the long run. There is scientific research that establishes that it is harmful," Eva replied.

"How can one cigarette hurt me?" Alice wanted to know.

"By leading you to a second and to a third, and so on, and so on, ad infinitum."

"You're using big words again, Eva," Alice teased.

"And you're evading the issue, Miss Alice," said Eva, annoyed because her deep concern was not shared.

_____ 1. foresight

_____ 2. belief in research results

_____ 3. lack of concern

_____ 4. questioning

_____ 5. caring

_____ 6. evading issue

_____ 7. affectionate

_____ 8. carefree

_____ 9. seriousness

_____ 10. logical

_____ 11. light-heartedness

_____ 12. risk-taking

CREATIVE READING   **D. Understands Settings: Social, Economic, and Educational**

DIRECTIONS: Read the following carefully. Classify each setting as social, economic, or educational by writing the appropriate letter in the space before each statement.

a. social   b. economic   c. educational

_____ 1. Small cars, big cars, pickup trucks, vans, station wagons. The long, seemingly endless line did have an end: a gasoline station.

_____ 2. As the curtain fell, the audience rose and filled the theater with thunderous applause.

_____ 3. The door marked "Board Room" opened upon a large room whose principal piece of furniture was a huge table surrounded by a dozen or so upholstered arm chairs. On the walls, pictures of company buildings and former company presidents stood watch.

_____ 4. After entering a dark and progressively colder passageway, they came upon a dimly lighted scene, a log cabin in the woods before which young Abe was splitting rails. Bent over, his axe in the wood, the waxen image looked like it would straighten up any minute, ready for the next blow.

_____ 5. We sat in a semicircle in front of a huge stone fireplace, the only light coming from the massive logs ablaze, when suddenly someone started singing.

_____ 6. Fascinated, they went slowly around the room to each of the large display windows that lined it and behind which exotic animals, some in pairs, some with their young, stood in replicas of their natural habitats.

CREATIVE READING   D. Understands Settings: Social, Economic, and
                       Educational

DIRECTIONS: Read the following carefully. Classify each setting as social, economic, or educational by writing the appropriate letter in the space before each statement.

a. social   b. economic   c. educational

_____ 1. They had seen quite a few on that long ride, those concrete constructions that resembled surf breaking, and always near them groups of young people either toting their skateboards or on them, waiting in line to pay for their admission to thrills.

_____ 2. Under a brilliant sun, seemingly made more so by the crisp autumn weather, they sat huddled close for warmth, jumping up now and then when pulled to their feet by the action on the field.

_____ 3. In the atmosphere, hushed by the carpeting in the aisles, clerks stood behind display counters whose own beauty was neither dimmed nor concealed by the exotic, expensive merchandise.

_____ 4. For the last time he was looking upon the desk at the front of the room, windows facing the door where he stood, chalkboards on the wall opposite the windows, neat rows of tablet-arm chairs, charts on the front wall.

_____ 5. Silence, the usual rule on that street, was broken by a car tooting its horn, dragging streamers, and rattling tin cans behind it.

_____ 6. By the light of a study lamp on his desk, the young man sat, his hands holding his head as if to ward off all interruptions, concentrating on the book before him.

CREATIVE READING   D. Understands Settings: Social, Economic, and
                       Educational

DIRECTIONS: Read the following carefully. Classify each setting as social, economic, or educational by writing the appropriate letter in the space before each.

a. social   b. economic   c. educational

_____ 1. Mr. Barry shook hands with the maitre d'hotel, who then led him and his daughter to his favorite table by the window overlooking the city, just as he had promised her for her birthday.

_____ 2. There were so many different departments listed on the directory. A "You Are Here" sign indicated that they were near the Space exhibit, which was exactly where they wanted to go!

_____ 3. Cars pulled into a lane just wide enough for one car and stopped in front of a window from which came a metallic box that opened like a hand. The driver dropped an envelope into it. The box retreated greedily to return in a few minutes. This time, the driver retrieved the box's contents and drove away to make room for the car behind.

_____ 4. From the outside, the building looked like a huge, windowless warehouse surrounded by acres of parking spaces. There were three elaborate entrances on different sides, all leading to a plethora of little shops and big shops, lining both sides of a wide, garden-like promenade.

_____ 5. The murmur of voices and occasional bursts of laughter led John to the door of the hospitality suite.

_____ 6. There were metal doors banging, young voices talking, yelling, laughing, books being pushed and pulled out of lockers. Some young people were pushing, some shoving playfully. Suddenly, all was shattered by that first bell.

CREATIVE READING   **D. Understands Settings: Social, Economic, and Educational**

DIRECTIONS: Read the following carefully. Classify each setting as social, economic, or educational by writing the appropriate letter in the space before each.

a. social   b. economic   c. educational

_____ 1. There must have been thirty to forty ten-year-olds whom four harried adults were trying to keep together on the platform away from the tracks. Excitement was making their voices shrill. Oh, the joy of learning by going for their first train ride!

_____ 2. Bob was looking for a white marble building with big Grecian columns. His errand had brought him to the U.S. Treasury Building in the large city. In the very narrow lane off a wide street, he checked numbers for the address he had been given. When he came to it, he gaped unbelievingly. It was a dirty, nondescript, gray business block with nothing distinctive about it to suggest U.S. Treasury except a very modest sign on the door.

_____ 3. "Room 316 to the left." They followed the instructions and came to a double door that stood open. They stopped, overwhelmed. The room, half the size of a football field, was lined as high as an arm could reach with rows of index card files. On the left were additional rows, perpendicular to the wall and with high tables in between to write down call numbers. On the right was the service area where the request slips were handled.

_____ 4. Trucks were lined up in parallel rows, their tailgates hanging, their doors open. In front of them, tables groaned under produce on display, reserves of which were kept in the trucks. People began arriving. It was farmers' market day.

_____ 5. Music was blaring forth in jungle rhythm under lights flashing alternating colors.

_____ 6. The park, flooded with light, was filled with the biggest crowd ever to come to watch the home team in the finals.

CREATIVE READING   **E. Responds to Author's Background**

DIRECTIONS: Read the following selection. Select the answer that completes each statement below describing the author's background, and putting the identifying letter in the space provided.

Ah, those "happy golden rule days" of high school! A convent boarding school it was, a 300-foot-long, four-story tan brick building. The driveway led a quarter of a mile from the road straight as an arrow to a circle in front of the high granite steps. To gain entrance, there was an outside bell, more steps, another bell, and another door. Some of the boarders called it a jail. It did give one a feeling of being safe and protected. Now, coming to its golden anniversary, "sheltered" seemed more fitting. Watches had been unnecessary there. Rising, chapel, meals, classes, recess, "collation," study, bedtime, all were ruled by bells. There were rules aplenty. But pleasures too! The uphill, snow-covered driveway in winter made for perfect sledding. In the early spring, studying before the evening meal was enhanced by the sun setting in gorgeous raiment behind the Aroostook Mountains. Boat rides on the artificial pond in early fall gave way to ice skating when it froze. Classes? The teachers had been outstanding.

_____ 1. The author attended: a. prep school   b. boarding school   c. public high school

_____ 2. The school was: a. in the North   b. in the South   c. overseas

_____ 3. The school was: a. in the city   b. in a suburb   c. in the country

_____ 4. This was before: a. 1940   b. 1960   c. both

_____ 5. The students were in an environment conducive to: a. permissiveness b. discipline   c. no play

CREATIVE READING   E. Responds to Author's Background

DIRECTIONS: Read the following passage. Select the answer that completes each statement below describing the author's background, and put the identifying letter in the space provided.

It was unbelievable! It was frightening! The mill owners were going to sell the mill village houses at auction! Simple frame clapboard structures with ridge roofs, most were built to house two families, a few four. One that housed eight was called the "Big Block," while another, because it had so many units, was called "Noah's Ark." Would they have to move? How could they live anywhere else? This little village, with its houses on parallel Anthony and Boston Streets connected by Meeting and Arnold, this was home. No fences made the whole area circumscribed by the streets their playground—a hodgepodge of cinder ashes from the mill boiler room, patches of grass and weeds here and there, the square wooden garbage "dumps" behind the outhouses all lined up equidistant from the houses and designed to accommodate the number of families in each structure, and the clotheslines and posts from which flapped family laundries every Monday. What would it be like to leave all that? Where would they go? Years later, driving through, remembering was difficult because of the many changes, and she realized that the auction had been her introduction to fear of the unknown.

_____ 1. According to this selection, the author grew up: a. in the city   b. on a farm   c. in a mill village

_____ 2. The environment was: a. neat clipped lawns   b. no clearly defined yards   c. paved

_____ 3. The people who lived there were: a. property owners   b. mill workers c. destitute

_____ 4. Although showing nostalgia about the past, the author: a. had liked living there   b. had hated it   c. had wanted to leave

_____ 5. Geographically, the village was: a. in the South   b. in the North c. not specified

CREATIVE READING   E. Responds to Author's Background

DIRECTIONS: Read the following selection. Select the answer that completes each statement below describing the author's background, and put the identifying letter in the space provided.

A never-to-be-forgotten scene came to mind as the parade went by: a sunny fall Friday afternoon in North Carolina, neat parade grounds surrounded by red brick barracks, a company of women Marines, the first, in parade formation, marching to the music of a Marine band. In green uniforms, visored hats with the cord of traditional red, tan shirts and ties, and stockings and brown shoes, the women in neat, even lines vertically and horizontally, all in step, in time, in rhythm, marched tall and proud. That was a "goose-bumper" of a sight if ever there was one!

_____   1. The author spent time: a. in the Army   b. in the Navy   c. in the Marines

_____   2. The time had to be: a. World War I   b. World War II   c. Korean Conflict

_____   3. The locale was: a. in the North   b. in the West   c. in the South   d. in the Southeast

_____   4. They were marching: a. as part of their training   b. in an Armistice Day parade   c. for show

_____   5. The marching took place: a. in a city   b. on a military reservation   c. in a city street

CREATIVE READING   **E. Responds to Author's Background**

DIRECTIONS: Read the following selection. Select the answer that completes each statement below describing the author's background, and put the identifying letter in the space provided.

Windows on the right, a blank wall straight ahead, a blackboard with doors on either side. Within that space, over thirty high school freshmen sat at desks, waiting...daring. At the teacher's request, they left their desks to stand around the room. She called each name from the list of Latin I students she had been given, assigning a seat and noting it as it was filled. That completed, books were passed out, each with a paper in it with space for the student's name and the book number. Directions to fill out the form were given. Then, the slips of paper were collected to be recorded later. "Since the books are new," the teacher said, "your homework assignment will be to cover your book. I'll check them tomorrow." She then proceeded to demonstrate how to open and handle a new book. "Now, open the books to page 7," she continued, only to be interrupted by the bell for the end of the period. Her first class ever was over. She was asked later, "Were you frightened?" After a brief hesitation, her reply was, "I didn't have time to be."

_____ 1. The author had experience as: a. a secretary   b. a nurse   c. a teacher

_____ 2. She was a teacher of: a. English   b. Latin   c. Social Studies

_____ 3. The teacher was: a. unprepared   b. hesitant   c. well-organized

_____ 4. What is described is: a. her yearly procedure   b. her first class   c. her daily class routine

_____ 5. For her, meeting with her first class was: a. not frightening   b. very frightening   c. dull

CREATIVE READING   **F. Responds to Author's Style of Mood and Point of View**

DIRECTIONS: Read each of the following statements carefully. Then, indicate the author's *mood* by writing the appropriate letter in the space beside each *odd* number. Indicate the author's *point of view* by writing the appropriate letter beside each *even* number.

Mood	**Point of View**
a. disgust	a. petitioner, beggar
b. distress	b. someone who holds the opposite point of view
c. extreme emotion	c. one who loves life
d. anticipation	d. grateful recipient
e. indignation	e. an independent one

_____ 1. In her article in Sunday's paper, Mrs. Quirl does not speak for all of the members of the church when she writes about her religious beliefs. She is

_____ 2. acting like a child, petulant and resentful because the father she loves and admires, in not acting according to her expectations, is faithful to the stern principles tempered with love which have always been the basis of his relationship with her.

_____ 3. This is the reason I come to you, as difficult as it is for me to do so. I desperately need your extra help to solve this terrible and immediate problem. Will you

_____ 4. help me establish a special fund just for this unique situation? Even if all you can give us is a small amount, it will mean a great deal to us all.

_____ 5. "I don't care what people think! Let them think what they wish! They will anyway. What I am doing is none of their business and does not affect them in

_____ 6. any way. Furthermore, they don't really know or understand what I'm about or why!"

_____ 7. "What was the high point in your life?"
When my leader embraced me, saying that I had successfully and faithfully

_____ 8. fought for our cause with written and spoken word, and that I had been a loyal servant."

_____ 9. I can't wait to get up in the morning. Each day is a gift to unwrap, take joy in, and give thanks for!

_____ 10.

Name: _____   Date: _____

DIRECTIONS: Read each of the following passages carefully. Then, indicate the author's *mood* by writing the appropriate letter in the space beside each *odd* number. Indicate the author's *point of view* by writing the appropriate letter beside each *even* number.

Mood	Point of View
a. love, tenderness	a. passenger alone on a deck
b. peaceful contentment	b. a grandmother
c. deep anger	c. nature lovers
d. anger, shame	d. honest man
e. awe	e. one who has been insulted

_____ 1. They stood before the large picture window of their hotel room. Before them,
       Lake Louise was a mirror of deep, deep blue. As their gaze went from left to
_____ 2. right, the mountains, majestic in varied shades of green, feet in the lake, heads
       reaching for the clouds, were darkening to deeper shades with the approach of
       dusk. The quiet was palpable, the beauty was all-encompassing, the moment
       was sheer bliss.

_____ 3. Alone, the passenger stretched out on a deck chair of the cruise ship and
       contemplated the ocean. It was smooth, as calm as the well-remembered Mirror
_____ 4. Lake of her childhood. The ship glided through the water's stillness, seeming
       not to ruffle it. The decks were deserted; the other passengers were readying for
       dinner. Although she was alone, she savored the quiet, the solitude, but above
       all the smooth, smooth sea. She was to use the memory of it many times in the
       future to counter stress and anxiety.

_____ 5. Flushed, shaking, fists clenched, she blurted, "How dare you? How dare you?"
       She turned on her heel, leaving the passersby looking reproachfully at the
_____ 6. young man, dazed by the verbal blows he had received.

_____ 7. Too young-looking to be a grandmother, she was one nevertheless.
       Tentatively, she stretched out her arms to her son to receive his baby daughter.
_____ 8. She accepted her tenderly, lovingly, tears of pride and joy filling her eyes. She,
       usually always ready with light banter, was speechless.

_____ 9. "I will not, I repeat, I will not do what you ask. Fire me if you want. Throw me
       out of your office if that will make you feel better. But I refuse to resort to lying
_____ 10. and cheating, and that is what you are asking me to do. It's not only that I
       couldn't face myself in the mirror afterward. It's just that it's wrong, wrong,
       wrong!"

231

Name: _____ Date: _____

DIRECTIONS: Read each of the following passages carefully. Then, indicate the author's *mood* by writing the appropriate letter in the space beside each *odd* number. Indicate the author's *point of view* by writing the appropriate letter beside each *even* number.

Mood	Point of View
a. self-confident	a. very lonely person
b. sad and lonely	b. disappointed
c. critical but positive	c. antagonist
d. critical	d. arrogant egotist
e. depressed	e. recently bereaved

_____ 1. Nobody, but nobody, is a greater fighter than I am!

_____ 2.

_____ 3. Mr. Watt's article in your April issue surprised and saddened me. His statements are a loose association of ideas that do not bear up under logical
_____ 4. critical analysis. He offers no proof. His article serves no useful purpose.

_____ 5. Both stories, "Gee!" and "All Heart," are just great. The two are extremely well-conceived and well-written. In both, the message is worthwhile. I cannot
_____ 6. refrain from asking, however, isn't there enough pain, sadness, and misery in the world? Couldn't stories of achievement and of selfless devotion also be well-conceived, well-written, and carry a worthwhile message?

_____ 7. He sat at the rowing machine, going through the motions rhythmically but very slowly. Clearly, his mind was elsewhere. Yes, things were different. The
_____ 8. youngest child of six, he had been the only one left at home. He thought of his brothers and sisters, recalling memorable incidents filled with love and laughter. And now, their mother was gone. Her death had been sudden, unexpected. He was grateful that she had been spared pain. He felt a huge void. He continued the rowing motions slowly and aimlessly.

_____ 9. She felt so lonely. Something was missing but she didn't know what. Was there someone she could turn to? she wondered. Yes, oh yes, but what good would it
_____ 10. do? Whether with people or alone, she still was overpowered by that sense of isolation, of emptiness, of incompleteness.

CREATIVE READING   **F. Responds to Author's Style of Mood and Point of View**

DIRECTIONS: Read each of the following passages carefully. Then, indicate the author's *mood* by writing the appropriate letter in the space beside each *odd* number. Indicate the author's *point of view* by writing the appropriate letter beside each *even* number.

Mood	**Point of View**
a. contemptuous, angry	a. one who has been frightened
b. calm, dispassionate	b. one affected by a ruling
c. serious	c. ecological concern
d. indignation	d. hardworking taxpayer
e. quiet indignation	e. a professional

_____ 1. Down with Logan! He won't get my vote. If I had my way, I'd boot him out of office right now! Imagine trying to legislate all traffic out of downtown!
_____ 2. He's going to turn it into a ghost town!

_____ 3. I have just returned from a trip during which I carefully observed legal speed limits. We have been getting reports on radio, television, and in the
_____ 4. newspapers that most drivers are observing the speed limits and that statistics are showing a reduction in accidents and in the amount of gas used. The reporters haven't taken a ride down the pike in a long time if they believe what they are saying. We were overtaken and passed on the road by cars, trucks, and buses which then disappeared from sight ahead of us. I was unaware that certain vehicles were dispensed from observing the laws!

_____ 5. As a physician, I personally know of one accident involving a pedestrian with a bicyclist. For the pedestrian victim, the accident resulted in neurosurgery
_____ 6. during which his life hung in the balance and after which his convalescence was very lengthy and painful.

_____ 7. The lunatic decisions of the city fathers disregard the everyday struggles of the mass of hardworking taxpayers. They not only listen to, they actually reward
_____ 8. a small, vociferous minority. Will they ever wake up to our needs and end their madness?

_____ 9. To revive and then preserve the Hudson River's ecosystem, fragile because of the industry along its banks, these very industries will have to continue and
_____ 10. even expand what they are doing along conservation lines at the present.

Answer Key

**PART ONE
VOCABULARY**

A. Word Recognition in Content

Page 16
1. f
2. d
3. d
4. f
5. b
6. a
7. c
8. e
9. g
10. e

Page 17
1. b
2. a
3. c
4. b
5. d
6. b
7. a
8. b
9. d
10. a

Page 18
1. g
2. b
3. b
4. a
5. d
6. f
7. c
8. e

B. Identifies Compound Words

Page 19
1. drive way
2. sun deck
3. blue berry
4. cross bow
5. door way
6. light weight
7. dish washer
8. home stead
9. cheese cake
10. crafts man
11. camp site
12. left over
13. far away
14. center piece
15. no thing

Page 20
1. teaspoon or tearoom
2. plywood
3. heartland
4. airport
5. classroom
6. seashore
7. evergreen
8. hideaway
9. tabletop
11. minibus

Page 21
1. cutout
2. homemade
3. blacksmith
4. seashell
5. waterfall
6. everywhere
7. someday
8. campstool
9. peppermint
10. saucepan

Page 22
1. aftertaste
2. backyard
3. cornstarch
4. heavyweight
5. timepiece
6. nearby
7. bookshelf
8. sailboat
9. bedside
10. landscape

C. Root Words
1. Recognizes and understands concept of root words

Page 23
1. true
2. wrong
3. weigh
4. root
5. born
6. hang
7. habit
8. hand
9. play
10. expect
11. hulk
12. light
13. book
14. kin

Page 24
1. model
2. cease
3. hard
4. hair
5. sphere
6. hem
7. depart
8. odor
9. moon
10. come
11. land
12. late
13. wife
14. way

Page 25
1. sane
2. revere
3. break
4. lemon
5. coward
6. charge
7. hard
8. hand
9. mild
10. myth
11. camp
12. cycle
13. line
14. rent

234

Page 26

1. herd
2. home
3. well
4. meter
5. run
6. lift
7. judge
8. confirm
9. cannon
10. canal
11. month
12. grand
13. act
14. hand

2.   Knows meanings of common root words

Page 27

1. root: *audi*
a. capable of being heard, b. instrument to measure hearing, c. person who specializes in science of hearing, d. a hearing or judging; sense or act of hearing, e. graphic record made by an audiometer
2. root: *phon*
a. science of sounds of speech, b. nature of sound, c. science of sounds, vocal sounds, d. instrument to record and reproduce speech, music, and other sounds. e. one skilled in the science of speech sounds
3. root: *poly*
a. closed figure with many sides and many angles, b. practice or state of having more than one spouse, c. expression of two or more terms, d. pertaining to many arts and sciences, e. animal having many feet
4. root: *phil*
a. lover of wisdom, a student of philosophy, b. loving harmony, fond of music, c. one who loves and seeks to benefit mankind, d. a desire to help mankind, e. study or knowledge of principles that cause, control, or explain facts and events

Page 28

1. root: *ocul*
a. pertaining to eyesight, b. physician specializing in treatment of the eyes, c. adapted to use of both eyes, e.g. field glass
2. root: *tele*
a. message written far away, b. instrument transmitting speech from a distance, c. optical instrument for viewing distant objects, d. projection of a view or scene to a distant point, e. transmission of thought from one person to another without ordinary communication
3. root: *solid*
a. stable opposite of fluid, b. union in opinion and effort, c. to make hard or firm, d. state or quality of hardness
4. root: *sol*

a. small umbrella to ward off the sun, b. pertaining to the sun, c. glass-enclosed room or porch, d. times when sun is farthest from celestial equator

Page 29

1. root: *petro*
a. abbreviation of petroleum; in Europe, gasoline, b. to change into stone, c. drawing or painting on stone, d. stony, hard, e. rock or mineral oil
2. root: *gero/geri*
a. science dealing with aging and its problems, b. a governing body of old men, c. pertaining to aged persons, d. specialist in science of geriatrics
3. root: *ped*
a. pertaining to a foot, a foot lever, b. going on foot, walking, c. care of the feet, d. instrument to record distance walked, e. base, foot, support of a column, f. to obstruct, hinder, make slower
4. root: *cent*
a. period of 100 years, b. enduring 100 years, 100th anniversary, c. divided into 100 equal grades, d. wormlike invertebrate having many (100) feet, e. 100th part of a meter, f. 100th part of a gram

Page 30

1. root: *geo*
a. referring to the earth as a center, b. science of chemical compounds of the earth, c. science of measuring size and shape of the earth, d. science that describes and interprets the surface of the earth, etc., e. science that studies the physical structure of the earth
2. root: *photo*
a. art or process of making pictures by the action of light, b. pertaining to the relations of light and electricity, c. instrument to measure intensity of light, d. microscope combined with camera for taking photomicrographs, e. instrument to communicate sound by means of light
3. root: *sol*
a. a talk to oneself, b. game played by one person, c. state of being by oneself, d. one who plays or sings a piece of music alone, e. leading part performed by one person
4. root: *bio*
a. science of origin, structure, functions of living organisms, b. written history of a person's life, c. measurement of the probable duration of life, d. branch of chemistry that deals with living organisms, e. group having the same hereditary characteristics

Answer Key

D. *Prefixes*
1. *Recognizes and knows concept of prefixes*

Page 31
1. anti	6. blank
2. pre	7. en
3. blank	8. blank
4. co	9. pro
5. de	10. ex

Page 32
1. blank	6. ir
2. pre	7. under
3. en	8. up
4. dis	9. sur
5. blank	10. blank

Page 33
1. pre	6. en
2. pro	7. blank
3. im	8. blank
4. blank	9. in
5. ex	10. co

Page 34
1. en	6. co
2. blank	7. blank
3. dis	8. dis
4. inter	9. blank
5. pre	10. anti

2. *Knows meanings of common prefixes*

Page 35
1. co	9. de
2. anti	10. pro
3. ex	11. dis
4. pre	12. trans
5. dis	13. anti
6. de	14. en
7. en	15. un
8. pro	

Page 36
1. un	a. il
2. pre	b. ir
3. anti	c. in
4. pre	d. un
5. pro	e. im
6. un	f. in
7. ex	g. ir
8. dis	h. un
9. co	i. il
10. de	j. im
11. de	k. im
12. en	l. ir

Page 37
1. defrost	6. proceed
2. encircle (d)	7. premature
3. coexist	8. antidote
4. exhale	9. unfit
5. unsafe	10. preset

Page 38   1. put off for after, later, 2. think less, think it under what it is, 3. roads

Page 38   underground, 4. lack of, bad fortune, 5. flow over its banks, 6. no employment, 7. being in, 8. across ocean, 9. to have someone do over and above what he did, 10. sailing around

E. *Suffixes*
1. *Recognizes and knows concept of suffixes*

Page 39
1. ly	6. none
2. ize	7. an
3. none	8. ship
4. ment	9. none
5. ible	10. less

Page 40
1. ment	6. ish
2. none	7. able
3. ive	8. none
4. ly	9. ory
5. none	10. e

Page 41
1. ship	6. none
2. none	7. able
3. ist	8. en
4. none	9. al
5. ive	10. ary

Page 42
1. less	6. none
2. ous	7. ness
3. ary	8. ly
4. man	9. none
5. hood	10. none

2. *Knows meanings of common suffixes*

Page 43
1. ous	6. less
2. hood	7. ive
3. ness	8. ous
4. ment	9. ful
5. ly	10. ee

Page 44
1. hood	6. ist (pianist)
2. ous	7. ly
3. ary (aviary; apiary)	8. ive (active)
4. less	9. ness
5. ment	10. ship

Page 45
1. ship	6. ness
2. hood	7. ous
3. less	8. ment
4. ist	9. ship
5. ive	10. ble

Page 46
1. nominee	6. flutist
2. aimless	7. solicitous
3. conservative	8. harmful
4. directness	9. shorten
5. employment	10. debatable

F. *Knows Meanings of Terms in Vocabulary of Language*
1. *Simile, Metaphor*

Page 47
1. S	6. S
2. S	7. M
3. M	8. M
4. M	9. S
5. S	10. M

Page 48
1. M	6. S
2. M	7. S
3. S	8. M
4. S	9. M
5. M	10. S

Page 49
1. S	6. M
2. M	7. M
3. M	8. S
4. M	9. S
5. S	10. S

Page 50
1. M, thirsty earth gulped down the torrential rain
2. M, world's tallest building touched the sky
3. M, set in a fiery furnace glow
4. M, frowned; let out a thunderous roar
5. S, as if someone had turned on a light
6. M, rooftops were a crazy quilt of somber colors
7. S, like dervishes walking on hot coals
8. M, time is a creeper; it is a jogger; time is a sprinter
9. M, he pivoted on his frustration
10. S, like a hook in the heart

2. *Antonym, Homonym, Synonym*

Page 51
1. A	6. S
2. A	7. H
3. S	8. A
4. A	9. H
5. S	10. H

Page 52
1. H	6. A
2. A	7. H
3. S	8. A
4. S	9. S
5. H	10. S

Page 53
1. S	6. S
2. A	7. A
3. A	8. H
4. H	9. H
5. S	10. S

Page 54
1. S	4. H
2. S	5. A
3. A	6. S

Page 54
7. H	9. S
8. H	10. A

3. *Onomatopoeia*

Page 55
1. none, 2. arduously, slowly shuffled, 3. swish, swish, swish of the window wipers, 4. repeated jagged whirring crowded out, 5. none, 6. rustled to the rhythm of her dancing, 7. now murmuring, now sighing, the pine trees responded, 8. buzzing of the bees busy, 9. mere ripple of applause, 10. muffled, mournful beat

Page 56
1. lonely baying at the moon, 2. barking, yelping, yawping, 3. half-detached muffler jangled as it played tag, 4. none, 5. chanting in wailing ululation, 6. merry, wheezing, tinny tune, 7. tanrantara, tanrantara, tantarara, 8. none, 9. bruising, beating, punishing your car, 10. glasses clicking and voices rising

Page 57
1. wailing sirens, 2. none, 3. caw caw of a lone crow, 4. long hissing of the slithering snake, 5. tired, worn-out, just putt-putted, 6. tintinnabulation of sleigh bells, 7. sputtered to silent immobility, 8. lazy drip, drip, drip, 9. ice beat out an abrupt tattoo, 10. intensified the pounding, blocking out.

Page 58
1. meows of the cats' concert, 2. cock-a-doodle-doo, 3. crackling, crepitant, 4. none, 5. scratching of a fingernail on blackboard. prickled, 6. weeping willows wilted sadly, 7. sleeping cat purred, 8. bombs bursting in air, 9. hit with a resounding crack and broke, 10. giggling gaggle of girls

WORD ATTACK SKILLS

A. *Knows Consonant Sounds*
1. *Initial single consonants of one sound*

Page 59
vow, view, visage
darling, daffodil, derelict
jangle, jail, jaunty, jury
follicle, fancy, fertile
master, massive, mayonnaise
nightmare, nominee, noble, noise
hearing, holster, headless
gorgeous, gadfly, gate, gorge

Page 60
solar, solicitude, sirloin, sixty
winner, wild, winter, would

Answer Key

Page 60 kicker, kitten, kettle
modern, mimic, modality, muster
lodestone, livery, listless, linchpin
jade, jargon, jack, joke
rousing, rivulet, roar, rue

Page 61 pension, puddle, precious, pansy
home, heredity, hike, hateful
salary, sour, salesman, sentence
balcony, balsam, bagpipe, bachelor
number, nurse, nunnery, novel
folly, foreign, facile
tender, tentative, tenacious, teacher

Page 62 care, consonant, cartoon
geography, giant, ginger, giraffe
bicycle, bottom, bothersome, beep,
    bother
kinsman, kidney, kale
pillar, pulse, pullet
tear
false, falter, fellow
lump, luncheon, lithesome, luster,
    likely

2. *Sounds of c and g*

Page 63
1. guy
2. calcium
3. give
4. cocoa
5. ago
6. gag
7. calf
8. decimal
9. card
10. music
11. digit
12. face
13. cob
14. keg
15. decide
16. region
17. giraffe
18. baggage
19. cane
20. goal

Page 64
1. gyp
2. cad
3. gem
4. danger
5. gaze
6. cage
7. geometry
8. critic
9. decoy
10. glad
11. deacon
12. cadet
13. gee
14. range
15. decamp
16. cake
17. ginger
18. bag
19. aged
20. camera

Page 65
1. cement
2. recite
3. go
4. fact
5. peg
6. circle
7. ego
8. cut
9. gauge
10. cylinder
11. cycle
12. tiger
13. cite or site
14. egg
15. golf
16. engine
17. gothic
18. cipher
19. sage
20. grief

Page 66
1. circus
2. gate
3. germ
4. cell
5. gentle
6. girl
7. code
8. age
9. digger
10. lag
11. cuss
12. geology
13. get
14. ghost
15. civil
16. German
17. gut
18. cigar
19. ecology
20. pigeon

3a. Blends

Page 67
1. fr
2. tr
3. sw
4. gr
5. sk
6. pl
7. kl
8. sp
9. cl
10. br
11. bl
12. gl
13. tr
14. dr
15. pr
16. gl
17. pl
18. br
19. sk
20. fr

Page 68
1. cr
2. fr
3. tw
4. sc
5. pr
6. sh
7. dr
8. wr
9. cl
10. gl
11. tw
12. fr
13. sp
14. gr
15. sc
16. wr
17. st
18. fl
19. pl
20. sw

Page 69
1. sp
2. sh, cr
3. gr
4. sn
5. gl
6. pr
7. dr
8. bl
9. fl
10. cl
11. dr
12. sm
13. br
14. pl
15. st
16. tr
17. sw
18. gr
19. wr
20. fr

Page 70
1. fr
2. gl
3. cr, st
4. gr
5. pl
6. dw
7. fr
8. br
9. dr
10. wr
11. cl
12. tr
13. pr
14. sm
15. gl
16. gl
17. sp
18. rh, st
19. sw
20. sh

3b,c. Digraph, diphthong

Page 71
1. empa<u>th</u>y, a
2. f<u>oe</u>, b
3. phos<u>ph</u>orous,
   a, a

Page 71
4. v<u>oi</u>le, b
5. fi<u>sh</u>, a
6. pea<u>ce</u>, b
7. <u>thrush</u>, a, a
8. jui<u>ce</u>, b
9. <u>ch</u>ore, a
10. wi<u>sh</u>, a
11. gra<u>ph</u>, a
12. s<u>oy</u>bean, b,b
13. pa<u>th</u>, a
14. sn<u>ail</u>, b
15. p<u>oi</u>son, b
16. <u>shush</u>, a, a
17. gl<u>ue</u>, b
18. s<u>oil</u>, b
19. <u>sh</u>uffle, a
20. <u>ph</u>armacy, a

Page 72
1. <u>ea</u>ter, b
2. it<u>ch</u>, a
3. ro<u>y</u>al, b
4. <u>ph</u>rase, a
5. qu<u>ail</u>, b
6. <u>sh</u>apely, a
7. d<u>au</u>b, b
8. <u>Shosh</u>one, a, a
9. c<u>ue</u>, b
10. <u>ph</u>antom, a
11. <u>ch</u>icanery, a
12. rel<u>ie</u>ve, b
13. c<u>oy</u>, b
14. <u>ph</u>ysics, a
15. <u>sh</u>ameful, a
16. t<u>oi</u>l, b
17. bons<u>ai</u>, b
18. <u>wh</u>orl, a
19. rec<u>oi</u>l, b
20. <u>sh</u>ore, a

Page 73
1. n<u>oi</u>se, b
2. <u>ch</u>ur<u>ch</u>, a, a
3. s<u>ea</u>, b
4. <u>ph</u>oto, a
5. p<u>ail</u>, b
6. <u>wh</u>ey, a
7. c<u>oa</u>t, b
8. <u>sh</u>o<u>u</u>t, a, b
9. rec<u>ei</u>ve, b
10. <u>sl</u>ush, a
11. <u>thi</u>stle, a, a
12. <u>ph</u>ilosopher, a, a
13. l<u>ie</u>, b
14. <u>th</u>erefore, a
15. cat<u>ch</u>, a
16. d<u>ai</u>ly, b
17. onomatop<u>oe</u>ia, b
18. <u>thresh</u>, a, a
19. cr<u>ow</u>d, b
20. c<u>au</u>se b

Page 74
1. c<u>ea</u>se, b
2. ba<u>the</u>, a
3. p<u>ie</u>, b
4. <u>wh</u>at, a
5. n<u>ail</u>, b
6. <u>rhythm</u>, a, a
7. t<u>oi</u>l, b
8. f<u>ai</u><u>th</u>, b, a
9. dec<u>ei</u>ve, b
10. p<u>oi</u>se, b
11. <u>ch</u>icken, a
12. <u>ei</u><u>th</u>er, b, a
13. l<u>oa</u>d, b
14. <u>wh</u>imper, a
15. <u>ph</u>onics, a
16. r<u>ai</u>l, b
17. <u>th</u>yr<u>oi</u>d, a, b
18. h<u>au</u>l, b
19. <u>ph</u>os<u>ph</u>orous, a, a
20. porp<u>oi</u>se, b

4. Medial sounds

Page 75
n: pony, goner, panic
y: haying, payee, halyard
l: ceiling, hollow, celery
t: footing, suited, sentence
h: inherit, behold, rehire
f: beefy, wherefore, infect
k: tanker, seeking, banker
g: maggot, cogitate, staging
d: index, candy, raider
b: debit, baseball, slumber

Page 76
f: careful, afire, befit
l: sailing, ailing, sailor
h: reheat, manhood, mohair
y: beyond, foyer, mayor
t: content, sorted, rotund
n: tenant, tonal, onus
k: ticket, looker, peeker
g: logic, toga, magic
b: carbon, debut, table
d: tidy, candor, under

Page 77
b: subway, rebel, saber
d: deeded, cinder, reduce
g: spangle, scapegoat, cogent
k: dicker, darken, beaker
n: tenure, connive, renew
t: continue, detect, cartoon
y: joyous, dryad, prayer
h: enhance, cohere, exhale
l: solar, polar, silly
f: befoul, before, surfing

Page 78
d: dandy, render, carding
g: rugged, digital, tango
k: breakage, leakage, drinker
n: tonic, lunar, anew
t: static, satire, party
y: lawyer, dryer, rayon
h: behead, unholy, inhibit
l: below, color, bailiff
f: infect, leafy, surfeit
b: timber, cable, bauble

5. Final sounds

Page 79
1. des<u>k</u>
2. cros<u>s</u>
3. flappe<u>r</u>
4. la<u>x</u>
5. none
6. none
7. thing<u>s</u>
8. fluk<u>e</u>
9. faul<u>t</u>
10. finit<u>e</u>
11. shining
12. del<u>l</u>
13. discer<u>n</u>
14. phoni<u>cs</u>
15. fat<u>e</u>
16. gap
17. son<u>g</u>
18. lot
19. none
20. bri<u>m</u>

Page 80
1. musi<u>c</u>
2. concer<u>n</u>
3. map
4. sin<u>gs</u>
5. lon<u>g</u>
6. sa<u>d</u>
7. mas<u>s</u>
8. mal<u>t</u>
9. lag
10. du<u>ke</u>
11. bra<u>ke</u>
12. none
13. linin<u>g</u>
14 drea<u>d</u>
15. refut<u>e</u>
16. pot
17. saf<u>e</u>
18. knel<u>l</u>
19. lyri<u>cs</u>
20. drye<u>r</u>

Page 81
1. fel<u>l</u>
2. prong<u>s</u>
3. las<u>s</u>
4. criti<u>cs</u>
5. lose<u>r</u>
6. li<u>ke</u>
7. defaul<u>t</u>
8. ur<u>n</u>
9. ta<u>x</u>
10. none

Answer Key

Page 81
11. fo<u>x</u>
12. ci<u>t</u>e
13. screa<u>m</u>
14. no<u>t</u>
15. saggin<u>g</u>
16. fer<u>n</u>
17. sa<u>p</u>
18. gon<u>g</u>
19. brea<u>k</u>
20. lul<u>l</u>

Page 82
1. fighte<u>r</u>
2. pell-mel<u>l</u>
3. thong<u>s</u>
4. fi<u>n</u>
5. none
6. gri<u>m</u>
7. sic<u>k</u>
8. bong
9. non<u>e</u>
10. gras<u>s</u>
11. sof<u>t</u>
12. nagging
13. physic<u>s</u>
14. ēar<u>n</u>
15. do<u>t</u>
16. mu<u>t</u>e
17. di<u>k</u>e
18. dreamin<u>g</u>
19. lap
20. pul<u>l</u>

B. Hears and Can Make Vowel Sounds
1. Long vowels, short vowels

Page 83
1. pāin
2. shē
3. lĕft
4. pĭn
5. fŭn
6. lōōn
7. fīght
8. mĭd
9. frāme
10. frĭll
11. dĕf
12. pōst
13. cŏt
14. līn
15. rĭb
16. mōl
17. mōōv
18. ō ä′sĭs
19. mō
20. mŭn′e

Page 84
1. fēēt
2. lĕt
3. cōld
4. rāid
5. lĕns
6. mō
7. mōde
8. mōōn
9. sēat
10. hōpe
11. sō
12. tūn
13. pōst
14. măp
15. năp
16. pōk
17. myōō
18. grōōv
19. līk
20. nŭn

Page 85
1. lōw
2. ōre
3. rāke
4. līme
5. gĕld
6. wrĕck
7. mōōt
8. fēar
9. pŭn
10. grĭt
11. mōp
12. ōr
13. găd
14. pĕk
15. lēch
16. myōōl
17. pē
18. gĭr
19. hĭp
20. găm

Page 86
1. lăp
2. plŭm
3. fĭckle
4. bōōn
5. fēat
6. gŏld
7. pēach
8. ŭs
9. lāme
10. mēēt
11. nūd
12. fōr
13. gā
14. ās
15. gŏlf
16. hō′bō
17. fĕd
18. mōōn
19. jōk
20. mŭk

2. Can apply vowel rules

Page 87
A.
1. ăsk
2. păd
3. bĕd
4. ŏdd
5. ĭs
6. dŏll
7. ĕgg
8. sĭll
9. nŏd
10. ŭs

B.
1. Hō!
2. mē
3. wē
4. nō
5. Hī!

C.
1. lē̸ase
2. cō̸at
3. dū̸e
4. gō̸al
5. bā̸it
6. mē̸at
7. fō̸am
8. nē̸ar
9. pī̸e
10. rū̸e

D.
1. māt̸e
2. nīn̸e
3. rūs̸e
4. vāl̸e
5. rōt̸e
6. brūt̸e
7. tōl̸e
8. gām̸e
9. nāp̸e
10. cōn̸e

E.
1. embărrass
2. ĭrrigate
3. fŭrrow
4. sŭrrey
5. sĕrrate

Page 88
A.
1. ĕtch
2. ĭll
3. ădd
4. ŏn
5. lăd
6. pŏnd
7. bĭn
8. ŭp
9. rŭt
10. hĕm

B.
1. bȳ
2. gō
3. hē
4. a
5. sō

C.
1. shō̸al
2. rā̸in
3. fē̸at
4. cū̸e
5. bō̸at
6. cē̸ase
7. fā̸il
8. lē̸ast
9. lī̸e
10. dū̸e

D.
1. lāt̸e
2. fīn̸e
3. fūs̸e
4. sāl̸e
5. dōp̸e
6. lūt̸e
7. cōp̸e
8. sām̸e
9. bōn̸e
10. pōs̸e

E.
1. squĭrrel
2. borrōw
3. fŭrry
4. dĕrrick
5. mĭrror

Page 89

A.
1. ăm
2. pŏnd
3. ĕbb
4. ĭf
5. lĭt
6. lăck
7. lŭsh
8. bĕt
9. ŏpt
10. fĭn

B.
1. sō
2. shȳ
3. dō (in music)
4. lō!
5. pī (in math)

C.
1. dīe̸
2. glōa̸t
3. lēad
4. tīe̸
5. mōa̸n
6. glūe̸
7. bāi̸l
8. fōa̸l
9. fēa̸st
10. ēa̸r

D.
1. dāte̸
2. tīme̸
3. mīre̸
4. pōpe̸
5. cūte̸
6. rōse̸
7. pāge̸
8. pāle̸
9. lōne̸
10. thōse̸

E.
1. ĕrr
2. ĭrregular
3. bărrel
4. quărrel
5. fĕrret

Page 90

A.
1. bŭt
2. lŭck
3. păck
4. pŏt
5. dĕbt
6. ĭn
7. ĕlf
8. ŏft
9. sĭn
10. ăn

B.
1. yē
2. crȳ
3. drȳ
4. shē
5. bē

C.
1. rēe̸d
2. hūe̸
3. mōa̸t
4. bēa̸k
5. bēa̸st
6. tōa̸st
7. fīe̸
8. wōe̸
9. rōa̸n
10. māi̸l

D.
1. cōpe̸
2. nōte̸
3. gāte̸
4. wīne̸
5. gāle̸
6. dōze̸
7. wāge̸
8. dāme̸
9. ūse̸
10. hōpe̸

E.
1. ĕrror
2. hŭrry
3. mĕrry
4. sŏrrel
5. părry

C. Knows Elements of Syllabication
1. Knows rules

Page 91
1. e
2. f
3 d
4. g
5. b
6. j
7. a
8. h
9. c
10. i

Page 92
1. c
2. a
3. j
4. b
5. e
6. i
7. h
8. f
9. d
10. g

Page 93
1. d
2. e
3. a
4. b
5. f
6. h
7. c
8. g
9. i
10. j

Page 94
1. d
2. b
3. h
4. j
5. i
6. g
7. e
8. c
9. a
10. f

2. Can apply rules of syllabication

Page 95

A.
1. e/ther
2. se/cede
3. pas/sive
4. par/ent
5. fol/li/cle
6. trans/fer/ence
7. set/tee
8. ly/ric
9. im/pair/ment
10. u/surp

B.
11. a/mass
12. per/form
13. car/a/vel
14. raf/fle
15. de/fer/ral
16. ef/fort
17. be/low
18. re/fer
19. em/blem
20. ge/ni/us

C.
21. ham/mer
22. a/bide
23. e/clipse
24. tri/par/tite
25. on/ly
26. myr/tle
27. pe/can
28. for/ti/fy
29. pub/lic
30. run/ning

Page 96
1. pur/vey
2. i/o/dine
3. se/ri/ous
4. lead/er/ship
5. re/ces/sion
6. mem/ber/ship
7. siz/zle
8. par/a/ble
9. pam/phlet
10. mi/rage
11. o/pi/ate
12. co/ex/ist

Page 97
1. in/fer/ence
2. key/note
3. hus/band
4. hal/yard
5. e/mo/tion
6. dis/tant
7. con/ven/tion
8. ca/da/ver
9. an/ti/bod/y
10. gen/tile
11. in/side
12. learn/ing
13. jan/gle
14. pre/vent

Page 98
1. ken/nel
2. hur/tle
3. hal/lu/ci/nate
4. em/ploy/er
5. e/mer/gent
6. dis/till
7. con/tra/ry
8. be/speak
9. an/chor
10. ge/nus
11. il/lu/mi/nate
12. res/i/dent

Answer Key

Page 98   13. shak/er   15. leak/age
             14. spec/trum

D. Uses Accent Properly
1. Knows and applies rules

Page 99   1. d, man'/ner/less   11. b, d, em/bold'/en
             2. a, be/moan'   12. a, b, re/ view'
             3. b, f, en/ti/'tle   13. b, pre/serve'
             4. b, d, nom'/i/nate   14. a, b, d,

in/cen'/tive

             5. d, e/ras'/er   15. d, du/al'/i/ty
             6. b, d, f, eat'/a/ble 16. b, bet'/ter
             7. b, de'/coy   17. b, d,

man'/ner/ism

             8. a, a/gree'   18. a, a/kin'
             9. b, d, jus'/ti/fy   19. b, or'/a/tor
            10. a, de/fend'   20. b, d, rent'/al

Page 100 1. a, de/cease'
             2. b, d, boun'/ti/ful
             3. b, in/crease' (v.)
             4. b, prom'/ise
             5. b, ex/plain'
             6. c, dai'/sy
             7. b, d, bet'/ter/ment
             8. b, pro/pel'
             9. b, sen'/ate
            10. b, d, na'/tion/al
            11. b, f, frag'/ile
            12. b, c, on'/ly
            13. b, c, bus'/y
            14. b, pul'/pit
            15. b, c, guil'/ty
            16. b, d, fa'/ther/hood
            17. b, pre/vent'
            18. b, can'/did
            19. b, f, sen'/si/ble
            20. b, f, chron'/i/cle

Page 101 1. b, punc'/ture
             2. b, c, mood'/y
             3. b, f, or'/a/cle
             4. a, re/deem'
             5. b, me'/di/ate
             6. a, de/ceive'
             7. b, d, nau'/ti/cal
             8. b, c, can'/dy
             9. b, f, o'/gle
            10. b, pre/pay'
            11. b, or'/ange
            12. d, e/mer'/gen/cy
            13. a, be/quest'
            14. a, a/bout'
            15. d, e/rup'/tion
            16. d, i/de'/al/ize
            17. b, ob/ject'(v.)
            18. b, o'/ri/ole
            19. b, o'/pal
            20. a, de/mean'

Page 102 1. e/rect'   3. a/part'
             2. be/lieve'   4. pu'/ny

Page 102 5. re'/cent   23. in'/ci/dent
             6. un/cut'   24. ex/ist'
             7. in/stall'/ment   25. se/cede'
             8. hab'/it/a/ble   26. sig'/nal
             9. jus'/ti/fy   27. cir'/cle
            10. in/cred'/i/ble   28. car'/ry
            11. re/fine'   29. lum'/ber/man
            12. or'/a/cle   30. i'/ci/cle
            13. syl'/la/ble   31. de/rive'
            14. tri'/fle   32. la'/zy
            15. sell'/er   33. sched'/ule
            16. sub/sist'   34. in/vent'
            17. co/opt'   35. lit'/tle
            18. gal'/lant/ry   36. un/scram'/ble
            19. ed'/i/tor   37. jea'/lous/y
            20. fash'/ion   38. beat'/a/ble
            21. pre/side'   39. east'/er/ly
            22. re/quest'   40. a/mend'

2. Can shift accent and change use of word

Page 103 1. con'/sort   6. con/tract'
             2. con/sort'   7. con'/duct
             3. con'/tent   8. con/duct'
             4. con/tent'   9. en'/ve/lope
             5. con'/tract 10. en/vel'/op

Page 104 1. com'/bine   6. pro/gress'
             2. com/bine'   7. pro/ject'
             3. reb'/el   8. proj'/ect
             4. Re/bel'   9. con/vert'
             5. prog'/ress 10. con'/vert

Page 105 1. con/test'   6. con'/verse
             2. con'/test   7. con'/vict
             3. rec'/ords   8. con/victs'
             4. re/cord'   9. con'/trast
             5. con/verse' 10. con/trast'

Page 106 1. con/script' 6. pro/duce'
             2. con'/script 7. con'/fi/dent
             3. con/sole'   8. con/fi/dants'
             4. con'/sole   9. con'/voy
             5. prod'/uce   10. con/voy'

COMPREHENSION

A. Understands Structure of Story or Paragraph:
main idea, topic sentence, sequence of ideas,
subordinate ideas

Page 107 1. Missouri is flat country.
             2. 1
             3. 2, 5, 7
             4. 3, 4, 6, 8

Page 108 1. We must get used to doing things
                differently.
             2. 1
             3. 3, 7, 11
             4. 2, 4, 5, 6, 8, 9, 10, 12

Page 109
1. Geese are effective, efficient crop weeders.
2. 3
3. 1, 2, 6, 9, 10, 11

Page 110
1. Conditions could not have been worse.
2. 1
3. 2, 4, 7, 10
4. 3, 5, 6, 8, 9

B. *Can Repeat General Idea of Material Read*
C. *Can Remember Specific Important Facts*
D. *Can Relate Material Read to Known Information or Experience*

Page 111   Dentists

1. Dentists' number of patients declining.
2. a. Improved/better oral hygiene
   b. Fluoridation
   c. Economic state of recession
   d. More dentists than needed
3. Yes, improved oral hygiene would tend to indicate more people
   a. are brushing their teeth, taking care of them, etc.
   b. They are unhappy because fewer patients means less income and that can affect their way of living.
   c. Doubtful. They will certainly engage in some promotion scheme to bring patients in for preventive work.

Page 112   Rats

1. There are as many rats as people and they are dangerous.
2. They eat anything (omnivorous). They avoid traps. Have long, pointed muzzles and dexterous forepaws; get in easily. Multiply fast. Are attracted by food and garbage. Live where there are people. Hard to exterminate.
3. a. Because they carry dangerous diseases.
   b. Because they are clever, cunning, adaptable. They avoid traps. They multiply as fast as they can be exterminated.
   c. It would be dangerous but it's possible. Danger would be for other small animals, like cats.
   d. If cats or dogs ate the anticoagulant-drugged food, they might be likely to die, too.

Page 113

1. A page of history was recreated.
2. Declaration of independence only a beginning. Arrest of Major Andre after meeting with Benedict Arnold. Imprisonment, trial, conviction, execution by hanging. Accurate reproduction of costumes, conversations, speeches, incidents.

3. a. It was possible because there are good records containing all the information.
   b. They should or will feel that it has been around longer than they had previously thought; that history took place there.
   c. Because more senses were involved: seeing real people, the colors, the speaking, the noise, the excitement, etc.

Page 114

1. A new family entertainment park where the idea is to take part, to put hands on rather than just watch.
2. Outdoor activities in Land, Air, Water Courts. Indoors: Science and Game Pavilion. In restaurant, see dish prepared from scratch. Learn and have fun doing it. Creators of "Sesame Street" involved in this.
3. a. Yes. Because having done something, you had to concentrate harder on it and you remember it better.
   b. That it is probably as interesting and as much fun as "Sesame Street." It would be fun to go there.

E. *Can Follow Printed Directions*

Page 115   1. column 1: begin, book, eventual; jingle; column 2: last, material, meal, outcome; column 3: pencil, satisfy, unless, yesterday
2. A E I O U *or* a e i o u
3. Will depend on name of the student.
4. Drawing is of a cornucopia.

Page 116   1. parallel lines
2. Answer will depend on name of teacher
3. Whoever is president at the time student does the drill,
4. A rough sketch of a saucepan

Page 117   1. Answer will depend on who is governor; name should be in capital letters.
2. 12, 13, 14—15, 16, 17—18, 19, 20—21, 22, 23—24, 25, 26.
3. ambivalence, excellence, instantaneous, outrage, unsatisfactory.
4. The signature should be cursive writing.

Page 118   1. B F J P V v w x y z.
2. The word "excellent" should be in cursive writing, each one progressively larger than the previous one.
3. Drawing should be of a fir tree in a tub.

Answer Key

F. Can Interpret Hidden Meaning

Page 119

1. Unless you vote for me, there will be loss of jobs. Only I can provide jobs.
2. With people out of work and no money to spend, merchants, restaurants, etc., will all suffer.
3. Our new model car gets more than 20 miles per gallon.
4. If it snows before the weekend, if there's snow on the slopes, if there is skiing, we will go.
5. The picture must be of a dog.

Page 120

1. The strange business is making a lot of money.
2. She is so afraid of flying she would not even take a lot of money to do so.
3. I'll have the money I need to do whatever it is I want to do.
4. She is so beautiful, so lovely to look at, it makes one want to keep looking at her.
5. Put your troubles away, out of sight. Forget about them.

Page 121

1. Leave well enough alone. Don't go looking for trouble, don't cause trouble; it will come uninvited. If you go looking for or making trouble, you'll be in trouble.
2. There has been no rain. There's a drought.
3. He is not a millionaire; he's not rich.
4. He isn't the effective/forceful/persuasive/moving speaker Dr. King was.
5. Keep your options open. Don't center all your hopes on one thing or person.

Page 122

1. The audience was so touched by his words, it took time for it to react and realize it should applaud.
2. Children are returning to the classroom after recess time.
3. The teacher/principal appeared.
4. Be careful of your words and actions.
5. He really was a pianist and could play well.

PART TWO
COMPREHENSION

A. Interpretation
1. *Sequences events from multiple sources*
2. *Makes generalizations from multiple sources*
3. *Identifies relationships of elements from multiple sources*

Page 123

1. b, d, a, c
2. When nature is not in balance, trouble, damage result.
3. All have to do with the weather; one results from the other.

Page 124

1. b, c, e, a, d
2. They tell the story of the evolution of laundering or How doing the laundry has become easier.
3. They all relate to washing clothes, to laundering, to laundering becoming easier.

Page 125

1. b, c, d, a
2. These were stages long distance mail service went through or History of long distance mail service in a nutshell.
3. They are all related to speeding up the delivery of mail between distant places.

Page 126

1. c, a, d, b
2. Each represents a step forward in aviation.
3. They are all related to air travel.

4. Identifies author's purpose

Page 127

Author's purpose is to influence the reader to "make do" while gradually investing in worthwhile furniture.

Page 128

Author's purpose is to convince the reader that viewing fall scenery from a tourist bus would be carefree, afford better viewing, be more enjoyable.

Page 129

Author's purpose is to convince the reader that running in the hall is dangerous, could cause an accident to the runner or to someone else.

Page 130

Author's purpose is to give Isabelle directions for a trip that will take less time and be safer.

5. Develops use of part of speech through transformation of sequences

Page 131	1. a	4. b
	2. b	5. a
	3. c	

Page 132	1. b	4. c
	2. c	5. c
	3. c	

Page 133	1. b	4. c
	2. a	5. b
	3. a	

Page 134	1. b	4. c
	2. b	5. a
	3. b	

B. Application
1. Uses multiple sources for documentation and support for opinion

Page 135 Responses will depend on sources used and how students handle them. Several possible sources are:

Inland Wetlands of the United States, by Richard Hale Goodwin. Washington, 1976.

"Margin of Life," by R. Allen. *International Wildlife,* Vol. 7 (March 1977), pp. 20-29.

"Flood Protection and Control." *Encyclopedia Americana,* Vol. 11, p. 44.

Page 136 Responses will depend on sources used and how students handle them. Several possible sources are:

The School Cafeteria, by Mary De Garmo Bryan. New York, 1940.

School Food Centers, by Norvil Lester George. New York, 1960.

Page 137 Responses will depend on sources used and how students handle them. Several possible sources are:

"Revised Statement on Fluoridation," *JAMA* (The Journal of the American Medical Association), Vol. 231, No. 11, March 17, 1975.

Flourine and Dental Health, by Joseph Charles Muhler. Ft. Washington, NY, 1973.

"The Truth about Fluoridation," by B. Spock. *Redbook,* Vol. 155 (Sept. 1980), p. 51.

Page 138 Responses will depend on sources used and how students handle them.

2. Uses maps, graphs, charts, tables when appropriate in response to readings

Page 139 One sample is given here.

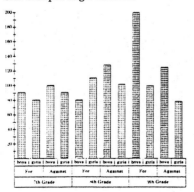

Page 140 One sample is given here.

Grade	School A	School B
K	205	190
1	250	225
2	275	225
3	280	290
4	302	270
5	310	275
6	340	300
7	310	300
8	330	290

Page 141

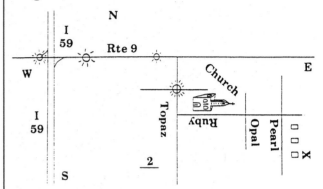

Page 142 One sample is given here.

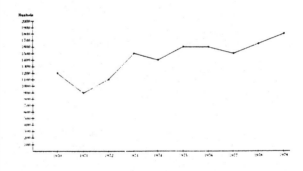

3. Takes notes during debate and other presentations in order to summarize and respond to logic used

Page 143
1. B 6. C
2. B 7. C
3. B 8. A
4. A 9. C
5. C

Page 144 Only answer checked: a

Page 145 1. A
2. He made good points, his thinking was good; his conclusions followed logically from his arguments.

Page 146 1. F 3. T
2. F

Answer Key

4. *Uses reading for different purposes*
a. *practical information*
b. *problem solving*
c. *recreation*

Page 147

1. b	6. b
2. c	7. a
3. a/c	8. c
4. a	9. a/b
5. a/c	10. b/c

Page 148

1. D, a/c	6. C, c
2. H, b	7. B, a
3. E, a	8. F, a/b/c
4. J, a	9. A, a
5. I, a	10. G, c/a

Page 149

1. G, a	6. C, a
2. F, b	7. E, a
3. B, b	8. K, c
4. A, a	9. D, a
5. H, a	10. I, c

Page 150

1. D, a	6. C, b
2. G, c/a	7. E, a
3. A, c	8. K, c
4. B, c	9. F, b
5. I, b	10. H, a

C. *Analysis*
1. *Differentiates between types of sentences:*
a. *expository*
b. *narrative*
c. *descriptive*
d. *persuasive*

Page 151

1. c	7. a
2. d	8. c
3. a	9. a
4. b	10. b
5. d	11. c
6. c	

Page 152

1. a	7. c
2. c	8. c
3. b	9. b
4. d	10. a
5. a	11. d
6. a	12. b

Page 153

1. d	7. d
2. a	8. b
3. a	9. b
4. c	10. d
5. d	11. b
6. c	

Page 154

1. a	3. a
2. a	4. b

Page 154

5. d	8. a
6. c	9. c
7. b	10. b

D. *Synthesis*
1. *Extends generalizations beyond sources*
2. *Hypothesizes*
3. *Suggests alternatives and options*

Note to the teacher: The answers for this objective are suggested ones. Should the student choose answers not indicated as the correct ones here, it is recommended that the student be asked to justify them. If such justification represents sound, logical thinking, it is further recommended that the answers be accepted.

Page 155

1. a. F	e. T	
b.	T f.	T
c. T	g. T	
d.	T h.	T

2. All checked
3. c, d

Page 156

1. a, b, c
2. a, b, c, d
3. a, b, c, e

Page 157

1. a, c, d
2. a, b, c, d
3. b, c, d

Page 158   Answers will vary with individuals and should be considered acceptable if they stand the test of being defended by the student.

E. *Critical Evaluation*
1. *Develops own criteria for critical review of materials*

Page 159   1. OK: a, b, c, g, h, j
2. OK: a, b, d, e, g, i
Original student criteria for 1 and 2 vary.

Page 160   1. OK: b, c, e, f, g, i
2. OK: a, b, d, e, f, h, i
Original student criteria for 1 and 2 vary.

Page 161   1. OK: a, b, c, d, f, h, i
2. OK: a, b, c, d, f, g, h
Original student criteria for 1 and 2 vary.

Page 162   1. OK: a, b, c, h
2. OK: all

2. Makes judgments about author's qualifications

Page 163
1. U	6. Q
2. U	7. Q
3. Q	8. Q
4. U	9. Q
5. Q	10. U

Page 164
1. Q	6. Q
2. U	7. Q
3. Q	8. U
4. U	9. U
5. U	10. Q

Page 165
1. Q	6. U
2. U	7. Q
3. Q	8. U
4. Q	9. Q
5. U	10. U

Page 166
1. Q	6. Q
2. Q	7. U
3. U	8. U
4. Q	9. Q
5. Q	10. U

3. Judges reasonableness between statements and conclusions

Page 167
1. F	7. F
2. T	8. F
3. T	9. F
4. F	10. T
5. F	11. F
6. F	12. T

Page 168
1. F	7. F
2. F	8. T
3. F	9. T
4. T	10. T
5. F	11. T
6. T	12. T

Page 169
1. F	7. F
2. F	8. F
3. T	9. F
4. F	10. T
5. F	11. F
6. T	12. F

Page 170
1. T	7. F
2. T	8. F
3. F	9. F
4. F	10. T
5. F	11. T
6. T	12. F

**PART TWO
STUDY SKILLS**

A. Uses Thesaurus, Almanac, Atlas, Maps, and Globes

Page 171
1. a	6. a
2. d	7. e
3. d	8. b
4. e	9. b
5. c	10. b

Page 172
1. b	6. c
2. c	7. e
3. d	8. d
4. a	9. a
5. a	10. b

Page 173
1. e	6. b
2. b	7. e
3. d	8. d
4. c	9. a
5. d	10. c

Page 174
1. c	6. c
2. e	7. a
3. a	8. d
4. b	9. a
5. b	10. d

B. Uses Variety of Media to Complete Assignments and Purposes

Page 175–178 Answers will depend on topic chosen, ingenuity, and thoroughness, as well as inventiveness of the pupil.

C. Uses Outlining and Note-Taking Skills
1. Uses outlining skills

Page 179
I. Purpose of college
  A. Growth
    1. Intellectual
    2. Emotional
  B. Preparation
    1. Career
    2. Life

Page 180
I. How to succeed in college
  A. Preparation
    1. Desire to go
    2. Desire to learn
  B. Needs
    1. Work habits
    2. Patience, perseverance

Answer Key

Page 181   I. Why more food sources are wanted
- A. Increased population
  - 1. More people—more food
- B. Environmental abuse
  - 1. Earth
  - 2. Sea
- C. Temperamental weather

II. Technology provides new sources
- A. Aquaculture
  - 1. Carp ponds
  - 2. Lobster hotel
- B. Hydroponics
  - 1. Food grown in water

Page 182   I. Gasohol commercially viable
- A. Rising cost of petroleum
- B. Costs of production
  - 1. of gasoline
  - 2. of gasohol
- C. Tax exemption

II. Reasons for optimistic future
- A. Results of tests
  - 1. Improved mileage
  - 2. Improved performance
  - 3. No engine modification
- B. Production incentives

2. Uses note-taking skills

Page 183   Notes must cover major points, similar to those given here.

Etiquette dates back to 1607
Dealt with behavior at court
Only for the rich and well-born
Is like attractive behavior
Good manners
Are relationships among humans
Being charitable
Respect for human and personal rights
No discriminating
With right attitude, rules unnecessary, behavior comes naturally, eliminates bad conduct

Page 184   We want a lot
There are prices to pay
Obvious price tag with tangibles
Not so obvious with intangibles
Yet real cost
We pay them willy-nilly

Page 185   To learn sportsmanship, goal of school sports
Fights during or at end of game, not so
Professional athletes give bad example
In victory, magnanimous
In defeat, no bitterness

Page 186   Hawaii is 50th state
8 major islands
2,100 miles s.w. of San Francisco
Honolulu on Oahu, capital
Largest island: Hawaii
High spots: Kona, Hilo
Pineapples on Maui
Garden island: Kauai
4 others, not as beautiful
Molokai, leper colony
Beauty abounds

D. Adjusts Reading Speed to Material and Purpose

Page 187

1. c		6. a	
2. e		7. c	
3. d		8. a	
4. a		9. e	
5. e		10. b	

Page 188

1. b		6. e	
2. e		7. a	
3. a		8. a	
4. a		9. a	
5. d		10. c	

Page 189

1. e		6. a	
2. c		7. e	
3. c		8. e	
4. e		9. a	
5. d		10. e	

Page 190

1. a		6. e	
2. c		7. b	
3. e		8. a	
4. a		9. d	
5. a		10. a	

E. Demonstrates Independence in Locating, Selecting, and Using Materials to Own Purpose

Pages 191–193   Since this is an inventory, there are no set answers. It is recommended that the teacher look over the student's inventory closely to determine if his or her self-assessment seems close to the mark. It is also recommended that the results be used to determine where the student needs individual help.

F Applies Problem-Solving Approach

Page 194   A. 2, 4, 1, 6, 3, 5   B. 4, 2, 5, 1,6, 3
1. Identifies
2. Gathers
3. Devises
4. Selects
5. Acts
6. Evaluates

C. and D. Mnemonic devices will vary.

Page 195 1. Source of the water
2, 3, 4, 5, and 6 will depend on the attack and outcome of what the student brings to the problem solving.

Page 196 1. Unapparent reason for condition of the tire
2, 3, 4, 5, and 6 will depend on individual problem-solving approach of the student.

Page 197 1. Necessity of getting to school without bicycle
2, 3, 4, 5, and 6 will depend on individual problem-solving approach of the student.

G. Designs, Uses and Revises Own Study Schedule

Page 198 1. D
2-12 should be As

Page 199 Checked: a, b, c, d, e, f, h, i, k
a=3 b=8 c=1 d=5 e=2 f=4 h=6 i=7 k=9

Page 200 Checked: a, d, g, h, k, l
a=1 d=3 g=2 h=4 k=5 1=6

Page 201 Any of the answers are acceptable. D, however, is a tested technique.

H. Locates Sources Within a Book by Using Table of Contents and Index

Page 202
1. III	6. Index
2. 283	7. Index
3. III	8. 159
4. 67	9. 233
5. Contents	10. French

Page 203
1. Contents	7. 24-hour
2. Comparison	system
3. II	8. Pronunciation,
4. III	Appendix
5. Index, 23	9. Yes
6. Index	10. No

Page 204
1. No	6. 7
2. Contents	7. 51
3. Index	8. II
4. Alphabetical	9. I, 40
5. Topical	10. Yes

Page 205
1. 18	6. False
2. III	7. True
3. p. 43	8. III, 48
4. III, 63	9. 57
5. Finder's Key	10. 28

CREATIVE READING

A. Recognizes Figurative Language, Dialect, and Colloquial Speech

Page 206
1. b	7. c
2. a	8. b
3. b	9. a
4. a	10. b
5. b	11. a
6. b	12. b

Page 207
1. c	7. a
2. b	8. b
3. c	9. c
4. b	10. a
5. a	11. b
6. b	12. c

Page 208
1. a	7. a
2. b	8. c
3. a	9. c
4. a	10. b
5. b	11. a
6. c	12. b

Page 209
1. c	7. b
2. a	8. b
3. b	9. c
4. a	10. a
5. a	11. b
6. c	12. c

B. Understands Literary Forms
1. Tales, songs, fables, legends, and myths

Page 210
1. b	7. b
2. a	8. d
3. c	9. d
4. a	10. e
5. a	11. c
6. c	12. d

Page 211
1. e	7. b
2. a	8. c
3. e	9. a
4. c	10. d
5. b	11. a
6. d	12. a

Page 212
1. d	7. e
2. b	8. a
3. c	9. b
4. c	10. d
5. a	11. d
6. a	12. c

Page 213
1. e	7. d
2. a	8. a
3. e	9. e
4. a	10. a
5. c	11. e
6. b	12. b

Answer Key

2. *Short story*
3. *Nonfiction including propaganda*
4. *Poetry, limerick, couplet, sonnet, blank verse, and internal rhyme*

Page 214
1. b	11. h
2. c	12. f
3. h	13. i
4. f	14. g
5. i	15. b
6. g	16. c
7. b	17. e
8. a	18. d
9. e	19. a
10. a	20. h

Page 215
1. e	12. g
2. c	13. c
3. b	14. e
4. g	15. b
5. i	16. a
6. f	17. i
7. h	18. a
8. c	19. g
9. h	20. c
10. f	21. d
11. i	

Page 216
1. c	12. c
2. e	13. e
3. g	14. a
4. i	15. e
5. f	16. a
6. h	17. b
7. c	18. c
8. h	19. f
9. f	20. g
10. i	21. d
11. g	

Page 217
1. c	11. g
2. h	12. i
3. d	13. f
4. b	14. h
5. f	15. b
6. i	16. e
7. g	17. a
8. e	18. h
9. e	19. g
10. c	20. i

C. Compares Value Systems of Characters

Page 218
1. B & J	7. J
2. J	8. B
3. B & J	9. B
4. J	10. B
5. J	11. J
6. J	12. B

Page 219
1. P & L	7. P & L
2. L	8. P & L
3. P	9. L
4. P & L	10. P
5. P	11. P
6. P	12. P

Page 220
1. P & L	7. L
2. P & L	8. P & L
3. P	9. P & L
4. P & L	10. L
5. P	11. P & L
6. P & L	12. L

Page 221
1. E	7. A & E
2. E	8. A
3. A	9. E
4. A	10. E
5. E	11. A
6. A	12. A

D. Understands Settings: Social, Economic, and Educational

Page 222
1. b	4. c
2. a	5. a
3. b	6. c

Page 223
1. b	4. c
2. a	5. a
3. b	6. c

Page 224
1. a	4. b
2. c	5. a
3. b	6. c

Page 225
1. c	4. b
2. b	5. a
3. c	6. a

E. Responds to Author's Background

Page 226
1. b	4. c
2. a	5. b
3. c	

Page 227
1. c	4. a
2. b	5. c
3. b	

Page 228
1. c	4. a
2. b	5. b
3. d	

Page 229
1. c	4. b
2. b	5. a
3. c	

*F. Responds to the Author's Style of Mood and Point
    of View*

Page 230

1. e	6. e
2. b	7. c
3. b	8. d
4. a	9. d
5. a	10. c

Page 231

1. e	6. e
2. c	7. a
3. b	8. b
4. a	9. c
5. d	10. d

Page 232

1. a	6. b
2. d	7. b
3. d	8. e
4. c	9. e
5. c	10. a

Page 233

1. d	6. e
2. b	7. a
3. e	8. d
4. a	9. c
5. b	10. c

Class Record of Reading Skills
SECONDARY LEVEL

On the following pages you will find copies of a Class Record of Reading Skills: SECONDARY LEVEL. This can be used to record the progress of your entire class or an individual child in mastering the specific skills at the Secondary Level.

The Class Record can help you identify groups of students who need instruction in a particular skill and to assess the relative strengths and levels of individual students. The Class Record can also be used in conferences with administrators, parents, and students to discuss reading skills progress.

Name of Teacher: _____

CLASS RECORD
OF
READING SKILLS
SECONDARY
LEVEL

Student Names

Column headers (read vertically):

I. **Vocabulary:**
A. **Word Recognition in Content**
B. **Identifies Compound Words**
C. **Root Words**
  1. Recognizes and understands concept of root words
  2. Knows meaning of common roots
D. **Prefixes**
  1. Recognizes and knows concept of prefixes
  2. Knows meaning of common prefixes:
E. **Suffixes**
  1. Recognizes and knows concept of suffixes
  2. Knows meaning of common suffixes
F. **Knows meaning of terms in vocabulary**
  1. simile metaphor
  2. synonyms antonyms homonyms
  3. onomatopoeia

II. **Word Attack Skills:**
A. **Knows consonant sounds**
  1. Initial single consonants of one sound
  2. Sounds of **c** and **g**
  3. Blends digraph diphthong
  4. Medial sounds
  5. Final sounds
B. **Hears and can make vowel sounds**
  1. Long vowels short vowels
  2. Can apply vowel rules
C. **Knows elements of syllabication**
  1. Knows rules
  2. Can apply rules
D. **Uses accent properly**

PART ONE

1. Knows and applies rules
2. Can shift accent and change use of word

III. Comprehension:

A. Understands structure of story or paragraph

main idea

topic sentence

sequence of ideas

subordinate ideas

B. Can repeat general idea of material read

C. Can remember specific important facts

D. Can relate material read to known information

E. Can follow printed directions

F. Can interpret hidden meaning

IV. Silent and Oral Reading:

A. Reads silently without lip movements

B. Reads silently at twice oral rate

C. Adjusts silent rate to material

1. Reads popular fiction at 200+ words per minute
2. Uses skimming techniques when applicable

D. Eye-voice span 3 to 5 words (in oral reading)

E. Reads aloud with comprehension

I. Vocabulary:

A. Increases vocabulary through wide reading

B. Organizes own word study techniques

II. Comprehension:

A. Interpretation

1. Sequences events from multiple sources
2. Makes generalizations from multiple sources
3. Identifies relationships of elements from multiple sources
4. Identifies author's purpose
5. Develops use of parts of speech

B. Application

1. Uses multiple sources for documentation
2. Uses maps, graphs, charts, tables
3. Takes notes to summarize and respond
4. Uses reading for different purposes

PART TWO

Student Names

- **C. Analysis**
  1. Differentiates between types of sentences
- **D. Synthesis**
  1. Extends generalizations beyond sources
  2. Hypothesizes
  3. Suggests alternatives and options
- **E. Critical Evaluation**
  1. Develops own criteria for critical review
  2. Makes judgments about author's qualifications
  3. Judges reasonableness between statements and conclusions

III. Study Skills:
- **A.** Uses thesaurus, almanac, atlas, maps and globes
- **B.** Uses variety of media
- **C.** Uses outlining and note-taking skills
- **D.** Adjusts reading speed to material and purpose
- **E.** Demonstrates independence in locating, selecting and using materials to own purpose
- **F.** Applies problem-solving approach
- **G.** Designs, uses and revises own study schedules
- **H.** Locates sources within a book

IV. Creative Reading:
- **A.** Recognizes figurative language
- **B.** Understands literary forms:
  1. folk literature
  2. short story
  3. nonfiction, including propaganda
  4. poetry. limerick. couplet. sonnet. blank verse
- **C.** Compares value systems of characters
- **D.** Understands settings
- **E.** Responds to the author's background
- **F.** Responds to the author's style of mood and point of view